Published by Live Well Publishing
Cover design by Alex McCarthy, Nomad Design
Interior design by Charlene Lucas, Fresha Creative
All photography by Elizabeth van Hulst,
less the image on page eight by Béatrice Cadoret
Leaf design used with permission by Vecteezy
Printed by About Print, 179 Vivian Street, Wellington, New Zealand

First Published 2016

© 2016 Lauren Parsons

The moral rights of the author have been asserted. All rights reserved. This book or any portion thereof may not be reproduced distributed, or transmitted in any form or by any means, without the prior written permission of the publisher, except in the case of brief quotations as permitted by copyright law. For permission requests, please contact info@laurenparsons.co.nz

Disclaimer

This book is not intended as a substitute for the medical advice of physicians. The reader should regularly consult a physician in matters relating to his/her health and particularly with respect to any symptoms that may require diagnosis or medical attention. Those who may be at higher risk (pregnant women, young children, the elderly or those with impaired immune function) should consult their doctor regarding consuming raw or runny eggs, raw dairy products or sprouts.

Cooking notes

All recipes refer to 1 cup as the equivalent volume of 250ml (8fl oz) of water, teaspoons (tsp) as measuring 5 ml (1/6fl oz) and tablespoons (Tbsp) as measuring 15 ml (1/2fl oz). Because fresh produce varies in size, texture and flavour, recipes should be used as a guide and adapted as required. Recipes include the following notes GF = gluten free, DF = dairy free, V = vegetarian.

Resources

Become a registered reader by adding your email at www.realfoodlessfuss.com/resources to receive the completed and blank versions of Lauren's meal plans, plus a blank weekly menu planner. You can then print, frame and proudly display this in your kitchen, writing on the glass with a whiteboard marker to plan your week.

Step by Step Videos

When you see the icon, follow the link to watch a step by step demonstration video.

ISBN: 978-0-473-36112-9

Find this book at www.realfoodlessfuss.com
For bulk and wholesale orders contact info@laurenparsons.co.nz
For daily inspiration join us on facebook at www.facebook.com/LaurenParsonsWellbeingSpecialists
Become a VIP subscriber at www.laurenparsons.co.nz/contact/become-a-vip and receive ongoing tips, recipes and inspiration.

for my children

In their words...

"get healthy, get happy and have lots of fun"

Lauren Parsons

 PLAN   COOK   ENJOY

The ultimate time-saving guide to
simplify your life and feel amazing every day.

Contents

Preface pg 8-11
Introduction pg 12-17

PART I

How To Eat Well pg 18-45

Why Real Food pg 46-61

PART II

PART III

Real Food Made Easy pg 62-75

Fresh and Delicious pg 96-115

PART V

Practical Tips and Tricks pg 76-95

PART IV

Tying It All Together pg 116-125

PART VI

Recipes pg 126-221

PART VII

PART VIII

Live Well Principles pg 222-233
Appendices 234-237

Preface

Friends and clients often tell me they don't have time to cook or to eat well. This book is all about overcoming that challenge. It shows you a practical, achievable, simple system that boosts your nutrition and helps you feel amazing every day.

You, or someone you know, may be in the same situation as countless clients I've coached over the years. A common story I hear is that in your twenties and thirties it was relatively easy to stay in shape but then as life has gone on, things have changed. Your waistline has expanded, you no longer fit the clothes you once did and you feel increasingly tired and lacklustre.

While you are highly successful in many areas of life, and give out so much to others, you feel like you've lost control of your own health. Life is so busy with work, family commitments and a packed schedule that you rely on quick fixes like takeaways, processed ingredients, and convenience food to get by.

Despite your best intentions you feel unable to overcome this growing problem, and the attempts you've made in the past have all come undone, leaving you feeling deflated. All the while your health is suffering and you are worried about your family's wellbeing. Maybe you even feel trapped in your current habits, and wish things could just slow down enough to get back in control.

I hear you! I know how busy life can get and how easy it is to put yourself last – sometimes even wishing you could turn the clock back and re-discover the person you once were. Well, the great news is that you can!

I want to show you how to make your meal planning, shopping and cooking incredibly easy and your eating incredibly enjoyable! I will teach you how to save lots of time and money and have several nights off cooking every week. You will never have to diet again. I'll even share how to overcome pesky cravings and how to develop a relaxed positive relationship with food so that you no longer feel it controls you.

How do I know that this is possible? Well, it's because I've been there.

At age 18 I packed my suitcase for a year-long exchange in France and had a life-changing experience living with a wonderful host family near Paris. I loved the culture and I adored French food. In fact I loved the food so much that after six months I had put on a lot of weight. My clothes didn't fit me anymore, my health was deteriorating, my skin was terrible and I felt absolutely miserable.

Then something changed. I began to notice that everyone around me was eating differently to me. While what we ate was often the same, how we ate it was poles apart.

Even at school where everyone received identical lunches, my friends would treat their food in a totally different way. Once I started paying attention, I learnt by immersion everything there was to know about the French attitude to food. I discovered how to overcome cravings and guilt and to fully enjoy my food at all times. When I stopped eating like a New Zealander and adopted the French's uniquely mindful way of eating, the excess weight I had gained dropped off effortlessly. My health improved and I returned home lighter and brighter than when I had left.

Sixteen years later, living in Canberra and pregnant with my third child, I was researching and planning to write a completely different book.

A nutrition book was not on the horizon at all. Then one day I got the shocking news that I had gestational diabetes. I still recall that phone call from my doctor and the tears that ensued.

In case you are unfamiliar with it, gestational diabetes is a condition that can occur during pregnancy where the placenta hinders the effect of insulin, which means that the body is no longer efficient at clearing glucose (sugar) from the bloodstream. This can lead to serious consequences for both the mother and child.

Fortunately I was able to manage it without having to inject myself with insulin, which would have led to several complications, particularly for the birth. Managing the diabetes naturally required close monitoring of my blood sugar levels, (a lot of pricked fingers), much more attention to the timing and content of my meals and increased movement at certain times of the day. (If you want to know more you can read the articles listed under gestational diabetes on my website www.LaurenParsons.co.nz)

Although concerning at the time, on reflection the diagnosis was a huge blessing as it effectively gave me a 10 week crash course in the life of a diabetic. Theory is no substitute for experience and I learnt an incredible amount. It brought home to me how much we can all benefit from eating to avoid blood sugar spikes, effectively reducing the risk of ever developing type II diabetes.

At the time I was also re-vamping my Get Fit Feel Fabulous online programme, creating recipes and introducing meal plans. As a result the majority of my recipes are not just healthy for the general public but also excellent for diabetics. I was literally able to test my blood sugar response to meals as I trialled and perfected them.

I started writing an explanation on how to use my meal plans. I also wanted to share what I learnt from the French and explain how to throw together instant salads. I added in time saving tips to make your meals flow. Then I realised that understanding the "why" behind real food was critical to motivate and underpin a commitment to lasting habit change. I pored over scientific journals seeking to understand the research behind various nutrition approaches. All of a sudden, I realised that what had started as a brief explanation needed to be its own book. What you are holding today is my complete philosophy and practical guide on nutrition. A lot of love, sweat and tears and an incredible team of people have helped me create it.

This book is the culmination of 16 years working in the health and wellbeing profession. It brings together my experiences living and working in France, my study of nutrition and bio-chemistry, nutritional coaching and feedback from countless clients, as well as personal experimentation in my own kitchen (and on my family!)

I wrote this book especially for the busy overloaded people out there who want to take control of their health. I hope it helps you discover a simple way to create time and space for more fun and fulfilment, all while nourishing yourself and those around you.

My Philosophy

If you already know me, you will know that one of my long standing catch cries is to

"Eat More Real Food."

While people often agree that eating natural, nutritious food is ideal, they don't always know where to start or believe they have the time. This book is designed to give you clarity about what real food is and how to get more of it into your body, with less fuss.

I've discovered that a great way to do this is by working smarter, not harder, in the way I organise our meals. I love efficiency! My strong dislike of wasting time and wasting food has led me to the meal planning system, and style of eating, that we now use at home.

International time management specialist Robyn Pearce once taught me these two principles:

"In order to go faster, first we must go slower."
"A small amount of structure leads to a great amount of freedom."

If you are caught up in the whirlwind of a busy life, I invite you to try a few days of going slower, absorbing this information and setting yourself up with simple systems that will ensure incredible long term success. Once your new habits are in place, you will be able to prepare nutritious meals so much faster and have more time and freedom for other things. Plus, I'm sure you'll love the food and how it makes you feel.

By following the principles and systems in this book you will

- find it incredibly easy to eat well and feel great as a result
- never fret over what to cook or what to eat
- enjoy and look forward to the experience of cooking
- never worry that food will go off or be wasted
- make your meals go further and be amazed at the difference to your food budget
- take great pleasure in eating and pride in what you've created
- look and feel fantastic inside and out
- most of all you will have great health, energy and vitality for life!

Eating healthily does not have to be expensive, or boring. My meal plans are budget friendly and recommend ingredients that are easy to source. I will show you how to save money that may have been spent on pre-packed meal components, baked goods and convenience foods so you can reallocate that money to real whole foods.

If you currently buy your lunch or snacks while out and about or get takeaways, you will save a huge amount by re-creating these meals and snacks through a bit of preparation and simple home cooking.

Even if you never eat out at present and already economise your food spend, I am confident that the information in this book will improve that even further for you.

Most of all it will give you a whole new way of thinking about food!

Thank you so much for taking the time to invest in yourself by reading this. My hope is that it truly transforms your life for the better and that by doing so creates a positive ripple in your world.

I'm excited and I hope you are too!

Let's get started shall we?

Introduction

Why is Real Food so Important?

The food industry has changed drastically over the past century. Food engineering, spraying, harvesting and processing have developed significantly to boost crop yields and extend shelf life, but not always in ways that benefit our health as an end consumer. There is a lot of research and debate in this area and, of course, much of what is presented is skewed by self-interested food manufacturers with large marketing budgets.

Throughout the Western world, waistlines are expanding and rates of nutrition related diseases such as diabetes, metabolic syndrome, cancers and heart disease are soaring. It appears that as we reach for more and more convenience items and highly processed foods we are eating ourselves sick. Never before have we seen such a high incidence of diabetes and its precursor, insulin resistance, than today. What used to be called "age onset diabetes" has had to be relabelled "type II diabetes" because children as young as eight are now being diagnosed with it. The statistics all over the Western world paint the same sad picture.

Our modern lives are contributing to the global obesity epidemic through a reduction in physical activity and the reduction of nutritious homemade meals. We rely too much on technology and so called "labour saving devices" which, rather than giving us more available time, ironically seem to have sped life up. We live in a "rushing" generation where instant gratification is the norm and we expect everything to be done quickly.

Our bodies, which are designed to move, are spending much more time sitting. Children spend many hours looking at screens rather than running around outside and we adults are much the same. While we are constantly complaining of being "so busy", it tends to be more of a mental rush inside our heads. We don't move our bodies nearly as much as we did, even just a few decades ago. The statistics show that a sedentary lifestyle (defined as six or more hours per day sitting) comes with a higher health risk than smoking, even if you exercise.

These long work hours and extracurricular activities create more pressure to get dinner on the table in a hurry. Cooking from scratch is becoming much rarer and the skills that used to be passed from one generation to the next are being lost. This rushing fuels a reliance on processed meal ingredients, convenience foods and takeaways, which tend to overload us with calories but lack nutritional value.

Where the natural whole form of a food once nourished us with all of its vitamins, minerals and fibre, these are often stripped away. The lack of fibre makes highly refined and processed foods easier to overeat as they don't trigger the same satiety cues.

They also spike blood sugar levels overloading the pancreas and leading to diseases such as diabetes. Alongside some of the goodness being removed from our food, additives which can negatively impact our health are being introduced.

Confusion Reigns

It may seem simplistic to eat like our grandparents used to eat, (and I firmly believe that this is what is required), but the reality is that it can be far from simple to do. We are constantly bombarded with marketing for products containing highly-refined grains, sugar, salt, fat, chemicals and artificial additives and preservatives.

Supermarket shelves are laden with products claiming various health benefits and it can be extremely challenging to know which ones to choose, which advice to listen to, and which food labels to believe. The prevalence of so much confusing information can leave people with a distorted view of what "healthy" really means. I believe we can overcome this confusion through education which leads to empowerment.

The Flaws of the Macronutrient Approach

All food is made up of the three macro nutrients; fat, carbohydrate and protein, with most foods containing a combination of each. In the mid 20th century fat was deemed unhealthy and dietary guidelines recommended people "eat more low-fat food". Note that the first two words in that statement are "eat more..."

Therein lies the problem. We have been eating more.

Rather than eating more vegetables or fruit, for example, we went ahead and ate what was marketed to us as healthy low-fat food. Food manufacturers picked up on the success of this marketing strategy of course and our shelves are now full of low-fat, low calorie and fat free options, packaged up in all of their various highly processed forms.

We seem to be obsessed with breaking food up into its parts and finding a culprit to blame for the obesity epidemic. For a while it was fat, now the spotlight is turning on carbohydrates or more specifically sugar.

The fact is, that there is no one macronutrient killing us or poisoning us. There are hardly any foods that are made up of only one macronutrient to start with. We have become so focused on maligning individual macronutrients (e.g. sugar and fat), that we have lost perspective on the importance of simply eating a balanced and varied diet of nutritious, natural whole foods.

Trends and Fads

There is a current trend towards rigid manifestos which fuel a climate of fear around food. Many people are opting for restrictive diets that cut out large food groups. These *can* give people short-term results, primarily because they pay more attention to what they eat and therefore either eat less processed food, or eat less overall. However, they do not need to maintain such a strict diet, lacking variety and cutting out major food groups. The same results can be achieved simply by being mindful, eating more real food and drinking more water.

We are even seeing a new eating disorder, orthorexia, where people try to maintain highly restrictive diets, leading to a negative food obsession. Ironically these people who work so hard to get "healthy," end up endangering their health by causing nutritional deficiencies, due to their restrictive approach. The deprivation mentality of strict eating regimes not only increases stress and emotional eating, it also makes life complicated on a practical level, particularly when wanting to eat out or share food with friends.

A Different Approach

I believe it is time for some balance.

Rather than being restrictive and citing a long list of banned items, we need to take a positive approach. Focusing on the food we want more of, rather than the food we "can't have" has a profoundly positive effect on our wellbeing.

Let's worry less about what "not to eat" and focus instead on getting more of the good stuff in! When you take this approach and fill up on life-giving real food first, the "not so good stuff" tends to take care of itself. By eating mindfully and eating a wide variety of real food you can cover all your nutritional bases while being able to truly enjoy your food to the full.

A happy medium is a place where you can relax knowing the majority of what you eat is super nutritious the majority of the time. Imagine adopting a healthy eating lifestyle you stick to for life, rather than a diet which, by definition, is a short-term period of restriction. Countless studies show diets ultimately backfire leading to yo-yo weight gain within 6-12 months. It saddens me to think of so many people struggling through this deprivation mentality only to end up worse off than when they first began.

How about we all simply eat more real food?

Try this formula:

- Focus on making real food a priority for yourself so that it is your default setting and the majority of what you eat.
- Eat a wide variety of honest real food, created just as nature intended it.
- Have a salad every day and drink loads of water.
- Be present, eat mindfully, smile, laugh and play every day.

Do these things and you will feel amazing. When you focus first on a good quality and an appropriate quantity of real food, your body will get all the vitamins, minerals, phytochemicals and fibre it needs, to thrive.

So What is Real Food?

I think of real food as being identifiable as having come out of the ground or off the tree and in as close a form to its natural state as possible. I recommend consuming a wide range of vegetables, fruits, wholegrains, legumes, nuts, seeds, sustainable fish and seafood, well raised meat and poultry, eggs and dairy.

Author Michael Pollan is well known for his summary of eating well which is to "Eat food. Not too much. Mostly plants." I wholeheartedly agree. When he says "eat food" he specifically means avoid eating food-like substances that aren't food at all as they lack any real nutritional benefit.

It is ideal to opt for locally farmed seasonal produce that hasn't been stored and transported for long periods, all the while losing precious minerals and vitamins. Where possible, always opt for foods with the least chemical intervention, and for organic, biodynamic and sustainable sources of foods.

The adage "you are what you eat" is true and can also be taken one step further when you consider the truth that "you are what your food eats".

Whether you are a vegetarian or a meat lover, remember that the nutrients that went into making your food will flow through into you. It is worth understanding where your food comes from so you can best nourish yourself.

In Summary

Convenience food can appeal as an easy fix at the end (or even in the middle) of a busy day. But with a small amount of planning and preparation and a few nifty tricks you will actually find real food more convenient and will see the benefits in terms of how you look and feel.

Your health is the most valuable thing you have. It is worth taking a small amount of time to set yourself up with positive food habits that will keep you in great health, for life. Our bodies truly are made up of everything we consume. Your beauty routine begins in the kitchen not the bathroom. The nutrients, antioxidants, and building blocks for every cell in your body all come from your food, and are essential for glowing skin, shiny hair, and to make you vibrant and full of energy.

Your best medicine cupboards are your pantry, fridge and freezer. It is the life giving nutrients in your food that support the correct functioning of your body and sustain your life. Everything that you eat has the potential to hinder or enhance your health, so opt for nutrient dense real food that truly loves you back!

As you join the real food revolution you can be justifiably proud that you are improving your family's nutrition and overall wellbeing. It really will enhance their lives, their brain power, appearance, energy and mood, as well as your own of course!

– PART I –

How to Eat Well

The Psychology of Food

Mindful Eating

Lessons From the French

The Negative Spiral of Dieting

Building a Healthy Relationship with Food

Overcoming Emotional Eating

The Effects of Stress

Great Digestion

Balancing Portions

Hunger and Satiety

The Psychology of Food

"Take care of your body. It's the only place you have to live."
– Jim Rohn

One of the most important things about improving your eating is to set yourself up to succeed long term. Any eating habits you want to establish need to be achievable now, as well as down the track. One key to long term success is developing a healthy relationship with food; one that allows you to overcome dieting and to feel relaxed, comfortable and flexible with food.

In my experience, it is the psychological side of eating – emotional eating habits and giving into cravings – that are the main reasons people fail to achieve their goals. Have you ever noticed that sometimes you know what you want to do, but just don't seem to be able to do it? You give in to unhealthy cravings? You overeat and then beat yourself up? This section will address how to build a positive relationship with food and free you up to truly eat the food you love and love the food you eat – guilt free.

Not What You Eat But How

Most people tend to start a health kick by focusing on what to eat, and even more so what not to. What I recommend, however, is before you focus on the *what* it is much more important to address the *how*.

Addressing how you eat is the starting point for real nourishment and happiness. The number one thing you can do to improve your eating, and as a result boost your health and feel fantastic, is to eat mindfully.

Mindful Eating

Mindful eating means paying full attention to what you are eating while you are eating it, and to how it makes you feel. Sounds pretty simple right? The challenge is that mindful eating requires us to focus and eliminate distractions. We are often so busy we feel pressed for time while eating or are surrounded by constant distractions. Many of us multi-task while eating; perhaps with TV, emails, social media, reading or even intense conversation, which means we rush through our meal hardly noticing what is passing our lips.

It's strange really when you think about it. Why would you eat a meal without paying attention to it? Think about the last meal you ate. How did you eat it? Where were you, what were you doing, were you sitting down, did you eat it slowly or fast, do you recall what each mouthful tasted like and how it made you feel? Why did you eat the way you did and is this your typical pattern?

Mindless Habits

Because food is available in such abundance, many of us have lost touch with our natural hunger cues. Rather than eating to satisfy hunger and waiting until we are hungry again we often eat purely out of habit, and can snack mindlessly right throughout the day. This is not ideal for our digestive health nor for maintaining a healthy weight and body shape.

Over time, we can develop eating habits that don't serve us; however, we continue them simply out of routine or because we've never tried a different way.

For example, we might associate food with certain activities such as eating ice cream while watching TV, snacking on cheese and crackers while preparing dinner, or eating potato chips on a long drive in the car. We might have adopted the habit of always finishing our plate, regardless of how full we feel or of routinely having seconds even when we are no longer hungry. We might eat lunch standing, talking, walking, working or doing several other things at once because we feel rushed and overloaded.

All these habits affect our digestion, our satiety cues and the total amount of calories we consume. It is surprisingly easy to adjust your habits if you choose to do so. All it takes is a mindful approach to eating which starts by being intentional about how you eat.

One of the best things we can do for our tummies and waistlines is to slow down when we eat and to focus solely on eating.

When we slow down and eat mindfully, we naturally regulate both the quality and quantity of our food intake.

When you pay attention to what you are eating, you naturally

- take your time and savour each mouthful
- feel pleasure and satisfaction
- have time to appreciate and be thankful for the food you have
- eat in a relaxed manner that leads to improved digestion
- slow down as your hunger is curbed
- easily stop eating when you are satisfied as you are aware of how that feels.

All of these things set us up to feel better, to eat in line with our body's needs and ultimately lead to total health and happiness.

Not only does mindful eating improve your absorption of nutrients but it also ensures your brain sends the correct messages to your digestive system, reducing potential bloating and discomfort. You eat amounts in tune with what your body requires. You notice the quality of the food and how it makes you feel and you have time to experience gratitude, which is a key to happiness. Overall, you feel much more satisfied physically and emotionally from the meal you have eaten.

Imagine every meal you eat tomorrow is eaten without rushing, without distraction. Picture how different it would be and how different you would feel. I can't emphasise enough what a **HUGE** impact this will have on your life! The best way for you to see that difference is to try it out yourself.

How to eat mindfully:

- Choose a relaxing place to eat, whatever that feels like for you. This could be outdoors, on the floor, at a table, somewhere with a view, on your own or with others. Whatever best suits you.
- Sit down to eat (always, always, always!)
- Eat off a real plate and use cutlery (unless it is highly inappropriate for the meal).

- Switch off all electronic devices large and small (or turn them to silent and put them out of sight).
- Remove books/newspapers and any other distractions. Eating is a single-task activity.
- Look at each forkful or spoonful of food before you eat it.
- Savour each mouthful thinking about the different flavours you can taste.
- Avoid starting the next mouthful until the previous one is finished.
- If you are conversing with others over a meal, take extra care to savour each mouthful and don't feel you have to rush in order to speak.
- Focus on the textures of your food - is it crisp, juicy, tender, creamy, crunchy?
- Pause a few times during the meal, place your cutlery down and simply sit. If you are typically in a rushing mode you may find this a challenge. I invite you to persevere. You can adopt a new habit!
- Be aware of your breathing throughout the meal. Breathe deeply from the belly.
- Aim for the whole experience to be relaxing and nourishing.

Once you adopt this way of being it will transform your eating and your life. I invite you to try it for the next three days. Pay attention to how you feel and reflect on the difference it makes.

If you have children, you can also teach them the same principles. I encourage my children to put their cutlery down and to take a deep breath between mouthfuls (and of course to chew with their mouths closed!) We also play games to guess what ingredients there are in things which is a fun start to food appreciation.

You may be thinking "that all sounds nice, but surely *what* I eat is still important". It is. Just remember that when we slow down and eat more mindfully, we naturally regulate both the quality and quantity of our food intake.

In short, it's very hard to overeat or to enjoy poor quality food when you truly eat mindfully.

As you start focusing on how you eat, everything will follow naturally and you will create habits that lead to effortless healthy eating. Positive change causes more positive change. As you continue to focus on *how* you eat, *what* you eat will change too. You will pay attention and be much more aware of how your food makes you feel. If you eat processed foods you will most likely notice they leave you feeling flat, lethargic and under-nourished. You will notice your body and soul desire to eat more real food that leaves you feeling vital and vibrant.

Lessons From the French

Here are eleven principles I developed after discovering the French way of life while living in a small village just outside of Paris. This was firstly with my host family as an exchange student and later returning there with my husband to work.

Living as part of a French family was an incredible privilege which allowed us to witness first-hand how the French shop, eat and socialise. Living and breathing the French culture has helped me truly appreciate the nuances of the French attitude to food and to understand how this can translate to better health for all of us.

These principles explain the subtle but distinctly different approaches to eating that are uniquely French. The "French paradox" is commonly referred to but much less well understood. How does a country that indulges in pastries, rich sauces and so much cheese remain so healthy and defy the international statistics? The answer lies not in what they eat, but how. The French have a completely unique way of eating, ingrained from an early age, and food is respected and treated with great care.

The following is my interpretation of the French eating habits. They provide an etiquette and approach to eating that I recommend we all follow.

1. Mealtimes are special occasions

Eating is about much more than just putting food in your mouth. Mealtimes are respected and celebrated as a special time. They are all about coming together and leisurely sharing the delight of food with people you love. Taking pleasure in your meal and enjoying the company of others is of great importance.

The love and care that goes into each stage of creating a meal is quite something in France. Every step from picking the best produce through to its storage and preparation is done with care and attention. Physiologically our bodies are best primed for a meal we have seen and smelt while it was being prepared. Home cooking creates a positive flow-on of improved digestion and increased nutrient absorption because of this anticipation of a satisfying meal.

Etiquette such as ensuring everyone is served before starting, eating slowly and at a pace that matches those around you, and having table conversation, are all vital to a great meal. We appreciate our food more when eating it with others who are enjoying the experience. I encourage you to reflect on this at your next meal and see what a difference it makes.

Even if you dine alone, you can still make an occasion of it. Find a lovely setting, perhaps outside or looking out the window and dine slowly. Savour and honour the experience.

2. Always sit down to eat

Eating is never done in front of the TV or computer, in the car, at your desk, standing up at the pantry or walking around. This simple but profound rule could just transform your life, or the life of someone you know. Picture how often we multi-task eating these days. Have you considered how little satisfaction you get by eating while watching TV or working at your computer, compared to when you sit and truly focus on your food?

Even for a small snack, take a moment to put it on a plate and sit down to eat it mindfully.

3. Dine slowly and savour the flavours of every mouthful

Meals are explored, appreciated and truly enjoyed. The French eat in courses, which slows down the whole eating process. Meals are always eaten with knives and forks while sitting around the table. The chef is acknowledged and the food is discussed with vigour. The different ingredients are savoured with each mouthful.

The discussion of the meal leads to improvements and ideas on how to make adjustments next time, perhaps which spices to add or variations that could be tried. This links to rule number one; a meal time is both a special occasion and a celebration.

Interestingly when we savour and relish the flavours and textures of a meal, not only is it more pleasurable, but we also absorb more nutrients from that meal. A collaborative study between Sweden and Thailand showed that iron absorption improved significantly when meals were enjoyed. Identical Thai curry meals were served to a group of women from each country, and the absorption levels of the Thai ladies was shown to be much higher than that of the Swedish ladies who found the curry too hot. Furthermore, when the same meal was blended to form an unappealing looking paste, the Thai women's iron absorption dropped by 70%. Interesting isn't it!

4. Have an entrée before your main course

This is part of dining slowly. It prepares your appetite for the main meal to follow and enhances the whole experience. Most entrées (called appetizers in North America) will consist of soups or more commonly salads with a lovely vinaigrette. Having an entrée before your main meal ensures that you consume a lot of fibre and nutrient rich vegetables.

If you make this one change to the way you eat, it will have a tremendous impact on your health. One of the few things that virtually all health experts agree on is the fact that we should all eat more vegetables. So having a salad entrée before meals is one of the most practical ways you can boost your nutrition!

Often we overeat on the meat and starch components of our meal. If you try eating a salad as a first course, with nothing else on your plate, you will find that you need much less of your main to leave you feeling satisfied. This protects your wallet as well as your waistline. Worried that you'll have leftovers? Perfect. I shall explain how to deal with those wondrous things later on!

An entrée at lunch presupposes a long lunch break, which is afforded to the French. However, as not everyone has this luxury my meal plans only include entrées with dinner. Of course if you do have time in your lunch hour then by all means enjoy slowing things down with this style of two-course eating.

5. Cherish simple flavours

It wasn't until I went to France that I experienced carrot salad or beetroot (beets) salad. While this may not sound like the most amazing revelation, when I was growing up, whether it was at home or elsewhere, I recall salads always being dry lettuce in a bowl with a few other vegetables and perhaps some dressing on the side. In France *une salade* refers to a basic green lettuce salad and it always comes coated in a delicious vinaigrette to bring out the flavour.

While one key ingredient may sound plain, it actually enhances your appreciation of that ingredient.

Eating one main ingredient (along with vinaigrette and perhaps some fresh herbs) allows you to truly appreciate its flavour and texture. For example a simple carrot salad really highlights the flavour of the carrot much more than a mixed salad.

You may enjoy trying out some of the simple salad ideas I explain further on. I invite you to reflect, as you eat these salads, on how much more of the individual flavours you are able to appreciate when they are simplified.

It also makes them quick to prepare and gives you variety throughout the week. You can still enjoy combinations of mixed salads as well, as do the French. I will explain my sensational salad blueprints in part V which guarantee a stunning salad every time!

6. Know when enough is enough

Enjoy your indulgences but keep them in balance. The French adore their food and take great pleasure in eating. They innately know that treats are to be enjoyed but over-indulging reduces enjoyment.

Rather than diet, French women simply *fait attention* or pay attention to what they eat. Instead of wolfing down a piece of cake or a chocolate biscuit with guilty feelings (as if the faster I eat the less it will count) they enjoy these foods slowly. They know they will balance the treat by having a smaller portion later, perhaps skipping bread at their next meal, or going for an extra-long walk that afternoon.

Michael Pollan, in his book *In Defense of Food: An Eater's Manifesto*, gives an example where, in America, the most common word association with chocolate cake was *guilt*, compared with French eaters whose most common response was *celebration*. This demonstrates how differently the French think about delicious food. They see it as something to be relished and enjoyed as a special part of life, not something to be ashamed of eating.

Imagine what a difference it would make if you no longer had guilty feelings about eating anything?

How much more satisfied might you be even with a small amount of a treat or celebration food?

7. Take a long stroll after a lovely lunch

It is very common in France to get outdoors and move after a meal, especially after a weekend lunch with family and friends. You don't need a particular destination. A walk around the neighbourhood will do.

The French tend to have an active attitude to life. They commonly take the stairs and walk to and from public transport or for small errands such as buying fresh bread twice a day. Interestingly, gyms and health clubs are much less prevalent in France than they are in the English speaking world. Staying active as part of your everyday life is the norm and is arguably one of the best ways to stay healthy long term.

Choose to adopt an active attitude and look for opportunities to move your body every day. New habits are easy to adopt when you start to make active choices in your daily routines.

8. Avoid snacking mindlessly between meals

This is something the French do incredibly well. Right from babies and young children, they are taught it is ok (in fact important) to be hungry and it is normal to wait for a meal. French toddlers are expected to wait patiently through pre-dinner drinks and four course meals as this is part of family life.

My family spent two months in France when our two eldest children were one and three years old. We got to experience the stark contrast between New Zealand and French dining culture which was often a challenge to adapt to (and a very good test of our parenting skills).

The French learn the importance of having a *bon appétit* which we often say in English simply to mean *enjoy your meal* but which literally translates to *have a good appetite*. Any meal is much more enjoyable with a good appetite and this is precisely how the French eat. They are in touch with their hunger cycle. They satisfy their appetite at each meal and then allow themselves to become hungry before the next meal.

Typically, they eat a light breakfast upon rising, a large leisurely lunch around midday and then nothing until dinner around 8pm. Children do have a *quatre heure* meaning four o'clock which, not surprisingly, is taken at 4pm. If it's only 3pm or 3.30pm and children grizzle or request food, they are simply asked to wait.

Wait is a very important and common word in all French parents' vocabulary. Only for some special occasion would you eat outside of these times, so people become good at exercising self-control. Practising delayed gratification is a good thing when it comes to eating, as it is for many things, and an essential skill to teach our children.

I'm not suggesting you should avoid eating altogether between lunch and a late dinner. It can actually be unhelpful to become so hungry that you are absolutely ravenous, as this can lead to poor food choices and overeating at meal times. Most people will find regular small meals beneficial.

The distinction is simply that when we eat, it should be a meal or a proper snack that you put on a plate and sit down to enjoy. This is as opposed to snacking mindlessly on all sorts of things at all hours of the day, which can make you feel like you don't know when to stop. The key is to get in touch with your hunger and satiety cycles and to follow these.

9. Buy fresh seasonal produce

Always go for the fruits and vegetables that are in season when they taste the best and are the best for you. This is also when they are the least expensive. Learn what is available locally and opt for that produce when it is in season. Many of us have lost touch with what is normally available at different times of year as we find the same produce for sale month in and month out. If you can get fruit and vegetables from local markets where it hasn't been chilled, stored and transported for days, weeks or months it will have more nutrients and goodness.

To the French, shopping is a whole culture in itself. They tend to shop regularly at markets selecting the produce that looks and smells the best that day. My French host-family taught me the art of respecting food, purchasing it lovingly, preparing it tenderly and eating it with pleasure.

10. Use quality cuts of meat

Again, choosing quality is important. It is better to have a small portion of premium beef steak than two kilos of low quality processed meat products. Things like pre-prepared patties, sausages and crumb coated meat-like products are often very low in actual meat content. When choosing sausages for example aim for those with at least 75% meat content.

Check the label! Many products are packed with surprising amounts of fillers that bulk them out as well as salt, sugar, additives and preservatives. This doesn't mean your shopping needs to be expensive. You can still opt for lower priced cuts of real meat which can be ideal for stews and slow cooked meals and will make your budget go further.

The French eat almost every part of the animal and know how to treat different meats accordingly. Learning a few slow cooker and casserole recipes can save you time and fuss and work well with your budget, as the cheaper cuts of meat become mouth wateringly tender after a day of gentle cooking.

11. Base desserts around fruit

Strawberry or mixed fruit tarts, blueberry or gooseberry pies, apple crumbles and upside down puddings are all common desserts in France. While these are still a treat, they are full of natural goodness.

After an everyday lunch and dinner my French host family would place the fruit bowl and small yoghurts in the centre of the table as a simple dessert.

For special occasions, and with guests, we would have a proper dessert, almost always based around a fruit, which was made with love and then savoured with the respect it was due. In short, you really can have your cake and eat it too! Just eat your salad first and appreciate every little bite, guilt free as you do!

The Negative Spiral of Dieting

Unfortunately, in Western culture it is increasingly normal for people to be on some sort of a restrictive diet. Even though research shows diets fail to work in the long term with the majority of people regaining weight in greater measure than they initially lost, they can still appeal to those who are desperate for a quick fix.

Physiological Effects

The challenge is that your body has a multitude of complex feedback loops to ensure its self-preservation. If you put your body into starvation mode it physically becomes more efficient at storing fat.

Drastic deprivation diets send the message to your body that it is in danger of a serious lack of energy, which could result in death.

To put it simply; your body does not want you to kill it. So if it feels it is being starved, it makes biochemical changes to become more efficient at lipogenesis (storing fat). It lowers the body's metabolism, so you burn fewer calories every day and have to eat even less to stay on track. It also inhibits lipolysis (releasing fat) making it more difficult to shed the excess fat the diet was designed for in the first place. All of this leads to much frustration and anguish for the unfortunate dieter, who struggles to understand what is going wrong!

Diets often lead to yo-yo weight gain. Dieting and weight loss can be misleading as people may see the figure on the scales drop; however, it is not only body fat that has been lost. Lean muscle and water are lost alongside the body fat which gives people a distorted view of their achievement. They may celebrate the number reducing without realising that they are actually shrinking their body's ability to burn fat.

> *It is crucial to understand that toned lean muscle is one thing you do not want to lose.*

Lean muscle is highly metabolically active (that is, it burns a lot of calories).

So when people diet, particularly if they are not doing effective strength training alongside their efforts, they end up reducing their lean body mass and hence have a much lower metabolism. This is all linked into your body's self-preservation instincts which you cannot override.

The end result for someone who has successfully lost "weight" but who has primarily lost lean body tissue (e.g. skeletal muscle) is that they end up worse off than when they started. Their body now burns much fewer total calories each day than it did prior to dieting. They are forced to continue eating increasingly smaller amounts due to their reduced metabolism. Further, when they end the diet and return to their normal eating routines, they are virtually guaranteed to put on more body fat. The whole process leaves them not only disheartened but also physically in a more challenging position to reach their health and wellbeing goals.

It breaks my heart to think of how this vicious cycle impacts on people's health, their confidence, their relationships and their entire lives. This is why it is so important to be able to kick the diets and the guilt, embrace real food and eat well for the rest of your life.

Psychological Effects

On top of all of the physical consequences diets create, dieting is very damaging at a psychological level. Diets tend to lead to more emotional eating, cravings, binge eating and result in a negative relationship with food that in extreme cases can control and affect people's entire lives.

Often dieters start out with a negative motivation. For example, they look at themselves in the mirror and are unhappy with what they see. This type of motivation can be beneficial to get you started. It can trigger you to take action to improve your health, however the challenge is that this negative motivation and negative focus are not helpful to succeed long term. The self-deprivation mentality that goes with sticking to a diet makes eating stressful and unenjoyable, but worse still are the damaging psychological effects.

Whatever we focus on increases in our lives. When you focus on the negative you tend to get stuck there. Sometimes without realising it, dieters can have a mindset of self-punishment for not looking or being a certain way.

Ultimately this links in to not feeling good enough, which is harmful and undermines people's self-belief. Negative self-talk can run rampant, resulting in negative words playing over in their minds and this works against them even further.

At a practical level, when we focus on all of the things we can't eat, we tend to find ourselves thinking about them constantly and craving them desperately. Our subconscious brain, which is the true driver of all behaviour, does not hear the word don't.

So if I spend all day thinking to myself "don't eat chocolate, don't eat chocolate, don't eat chocolate" all my subconscious brain can hear is "eat chocolate, eat chocolate, eat chocolate!" I am very likely to crave chocolate and to eventually give in and eat it. Then I feel guilty for giving up and eating this "bad" food which, in turn, makes me feel like I too am "bad". As a result I will feel even worse about myself which takes me back to square one.

Please don't take from this example that chocolate is a bad food! It can be a fantastic food eaten in the right amount, at the right time and in the right way.

Psychologist Dr Robi Sonderegger explains that feelings of guilt and shame are the most common precursors to relapse. In other words, if you beat yourself up for what you have done, you are almost certain to do it again. This causes people to get stuck in a negative dieting cycle and feel increasingly desperate to try anything to get out of it.

The key shift to make is to move away from a negative motivation (i.e. focusing on what you don't want) to a positive motivation (i.e. focusing on how you want to look, feel and be and what you want to be able to do.)

> Let's take Jane for example. Jane comes into my office and I say,
>
> "Tell me Jane, what is it that you want?"
>
> Jane thinks for a moment then replies,
>
> "I just feel so awful Lauren. I want to stop being this way,
> I want to stop feeling so flabby, tired and overweight."

When we pause that scene and consider what was shared, we notice that rather than telling me what she wanted, Jane instead explained exactly what she didn't want.

This is incredibly common.

We tend to spend a lot of time focusing on and thinking about *not* getting what we *don't* want, as opposed to getting what we *do* want.

Tune in to your own self-talk and catch yourself whenever you focus on what you don't want (we all do it from time to time!) When you heighten your awareness it is a simple shift to set your goals and intentions in the positive. Jane can choose to focus on what she wants which might be feeling fantastic, fit, sexy, beautiful, fabulous, stunning, gorgeous, vibrant, confident, energised or any other descriptions that line up with her true goals.

As soon as she shifts her focus from the negative to the positive, everything changes. Once her focus changes, her self-talk easily switches to "I am getting fitter and I am becoming confident". She finds it easy to make decisions in line with feeling fit and confident because that is the image she has in mind and her subconscious brain will line her up with opportunities that lead her towards that outcome.

Even better, she might choose to make those statements in the present tense, which is much more powerful. She can say to herself, I am beautiful, I am vibrant, I am gorgeous!

Can you imagine that?

Picture Jane as your best friend and think what encouraging words you would say to her.

Now, I invite you to say those things to yourself. You truly are your best coach, friend and confidant. Just love yourself a little more and take the best care of yourself you possibly can!

I am uplifted just writing these words, hoping that they are going to touch your heart and trusting they are going to make a difference for you.

Don't take this lightly. If this speaks to you then you truly are ready to let go of the negative self-talk that has held you back and embrace the positive new you.

This small but significant shift in thinking can literally free you from the negative spiral of dieting, deprivation and self-loathing to step forward confidently with a positive new focus and tonnes of love and self-acceptance.

This, my friend, is the best possible place to start any change of habit.

Once you decide to get off the dieting cycle you can

- feel confident in your skin
- relax about food and get past emotional eating
- get a variety of nutritious foods into your diet
- savour your treats guilt free, knowing that you're keeping things in balance
- realise that food is there to nourish you and to be enjoyed!

EAT the food you LOVE and LOVE the food you EAT.

Eating the food you love is about getting satisfaction from the flavours in foods you really enjoy. Loving the food you eat is about keeping things in balance so you feel fantastic after eating. Generally we don't feel great after scoffing a huge serving of greasy fast food or devouring an entire block of chocolate.

That is no longer loving the food you eat. Remember that allowing yourself to have a little of anything from time to time is part of a healthy, positive view of food.

It is important to understand that while some foods are much more nutritious for us (some are even held up as super-foods), other foods (which you might previously have labelled as bad) can give us great emotional rewards.

Eating is about so much more than just calories, so we need to keep a balance and enjoy eating our "sometimes foods" sometimes.

Who wants to be on a diet for the rest of their life?

Remember that rather than focusing on what to stop eating...

Focus first on getting good stuff in!

First and foremost, make it your default to include good nutrition in your everyday routines. Eat a wide variety of fruit and vegetables and high fibre whole foods and drink plenty of water every day.

Take the focus off the so called "bad" foods and let go of the guilt. When you do this you will find you can include treats without going overboard and simply enjoy them. You can also make them as nutritious as possible so they nourish your body and soul. This allows you to live life in the real world where socialising, eating out and taking part in celebrations are all part of the routine.

Building a Healthy Relationship with Food

A key foundation to ditching diets is to develop a positive relationship with food.

I invite you to play a quick game with me.

Fill in the blank – Food is _____?

Pause and ask yourself again.

Food is _____?

What comes to mind? Some might say: "yummy, energy, fuel, pleasurable, comforting, necessary, nourishment".

The way that we think of food differs from person to person. While athletes will typically think of food as simply fuel for the body, a more common theme for most people is that food is pleasure and/or comfort. When food is pleasure or comfort for you it's important to realise that reducing or changing your food intake will be a long-term challenge unless you boost your pleasure in some other form.

Just think about that for a moment. Have you considered how you can increase pleasure elsewhere in your life? Picture the little things in life that bring you joy and happiness, small activities you can do to restore your soul and make you feel content.

You might like to: get out in nature, take a hot bath, tidy your cupboards, garden, read, be still, go for a solitary run or walk, socialise with friends, laugh, play with your kids or pets, or sing your favourite song. Perhaps something different altogether.

What would be on your list?

Plan how you can fit those things into your daily and weekly routines. They will build your personal resilience and help you feel satisfied and at peace with the world. This stops you feeling like you "just need a little something", and heading to the pantry to see if it might just be in there!

Ideally it is great if we can move away from a relationship where food is just pleasure or comfort and see it as nourishment for our entire body. Keep this nourishment outlook in mind as you continue through this section.

Overcoming Emotional Eating

Imagine your eating habits are like an elephant and a rider. The rider is your logic and reason to know what you intend to do.

It's the part of your brain that says things like; "I'm going to eat really well all day", "I'll just snack on carrots this afternoon" or "I'm going to have a small helping of this and then I'll stop".

Then there is this large powerful beast that is our emotions which can rear up and take us off track at any moment. Before we know it, we are half way down a completely different path to the one we intended.

The emotional brain says things like: "I need this chocolate now, I just can't get through the afternoon without it, I shouldn't but I can't stop myself... Oh well, now I've blown it, I may as well finish the entire packet, then no one will see the wrapper!"

International expert on behaviour change, Tony Robbins, asks "Why do we do what we do?" He explains human behaviour is controlled by our emotions and not logic. The emotional part of our brain (the limbic system) has this tug of war relationship with the logical system of our brain (the prefrontal cortex). Unfortunately the limbic system tends to win the majority of the time, despite our best logical efforts.

We get stuck if we simply aim to use our logic and "try to eat better". Willpower will not cut it. Our willpower is much like the strength of the rider trying to physically steer the elephant; eventually that strength will tire and run out, so it is a resource we must use wisely.

The key is to learn how to direct the elephant in the direction we want to go so we can work with it, rather than against it, in order to reach our goal. We also need to get in touch with our emotional patterns and learn to interrupt and reset them when required to create new pathways for the elephant.

Our brain works via neural pathways that are strengthened over time to form habits. Imagine a field of tall grass. If someone were to walk across it from corner to corner they would leave a faint path. If they repeated this trip several times the path would widen and become clearer. Over time it would become the path of least resistance.

Similarly, our default habits are the easiest and most common reactions we have (for example overeating or eating mindlessly). Establishing new habits can take time as we need to strengthen new neural paths by practising the positive habits repeatedly until they are ingrained.

Direct the Elephant

Because the driving force for our behaviour is our emotions, to change our habits we need to focus on the emotional reward linked to our goal. This trains and directs the elephant to naturally want to head in that direction. It starts by choosing to focus on the solution rather than focusing on the problem. It is like programming the GPS of your emotional elephant with the right coordinates. Rather than focusing on what you don't want (as in Jane's example earlier on), programme the coordinates of where you want to be and how you want to look and feel into your emotional GPS.

To do this, it is vital to have a crystal clear understanding of your goals and specific milestones, and most of all, to take the time to truly picture how it will feel once you have achieved them. This is an incredibly valuable exercise to do before setting out to achieve any goal, as it is the secret to switch on your internal motivation. When your internal motivation is switched on, you cannot fail.

"Motivation is a fire from within. If someone else tries to light that fire under you, chances are it will burn very briefly."

— Dr Stephen Covey

Think about your personal goals and write them down in the positive. Picture yourself in a few months' time having achieved all of your goals and being in the best physical condition you can imagine. Think of some specific definable milestones such as:

> I will fit back into my favourite jeans.
>
> I will be able to start back into my sport again.
>
> I will enjoy playing rough and tumble with the kids/grandkids.
>
> I will feel confident wearing my swimsuit on holiday.
>
> I will be able to walk up the stairs without getting breathless.
>
> I will have great energy all day.
>
> I will look stunning in those family photos.

Picture your day-to-day life when you feel that way. Imagine getting up in the morning, looking in the mirror, getting dressed and feeling positive and excited about your day ahead. Imagine how confident you will feel about yourself and what a difference it will make to how you interact with people. Think about what effect it will have on how you feel, on your relationships and your overall enjoyment of life. Write this down.

Fast forward a further six months after achieving these initial goals and picture having even better health, and feeling even more vibrant and energised, and being able to do more things with renewed confidence.

Imagine what a day in your life is like now; picture all of the new things you can do, how much more you can relax and enjoy time with family and friends and how freeing it will be for you. Write this down too.

Get excited about the possibilities and just what an impact it will truly have on your life. Imagine how it will feel!

The best way to do this is to close your eyes and mentally play those pictures over in your mind. See yourself in the future in the best possible shape you can imagine, enjoying fantastic health and all that goes with it. Then, once you have pictured that and how great it will feel, come up with three words that best describe that feeling.

I invite you to go ahead and do this now! Reading this book and thinking about your answers will have very poor results compared with taking a few minutes to do this simple exercise, picturing these scenarios and putting pen to paper.

Please take a moment now to complete the whole exercise before continuing.

Once you have chosen three words to describe that feeling for you, write them down on a brightly-coloured piece of paper or on post it notes.

Put your three words on the wall where you will see them regularly.

This could be beside your bed, by your computer screen or on the fridge.

Every time you see those three words you will be reminded of how fantastic it will feel to have achieved all of your goals. You can even cut out thumbnail size squares of that same coloured paper and put them in places like your wallet, on your car steering wheel, by the kitchen sink and on the edge of your computer screen. Each time you see these brightly-coloured squares, they too will send this message to your subconscious and reinforce the feeling you have pictured.

This is called positive priming and you can read more about how powerful it is in Malcolm Gladwell's brilliant book *Blink*. The key is to prime yourself with the positive thoughts associated with where you want to be and how you want to feel, rather than focusing on where you are now, which leaves you stuck in old habits and patterns.

Because feelings are emotional and linked to your subconscious, they will naturally draw you towards the goals you desire. This makes it easy to make great choices in your day to day life because your internal motivation is now programed to head in the right direction. Your elephant will work for you and knows where it wants to go.

Having the clearly defined milestone helps you get through your moments. We all have moments when we could hit the snooze button and sleep in, or when someone offers us extra food we don't really need. We are much less likely to give in to these moments when we have the context of the bigger picture firmly in mind.

At an emotional level, the positive feelings associated with achieving your goals will out-weigh the instant gratification the poor choice would bring.

Simply put, you have a big enough reason to make great choices. After all, it is our small daily choices that determine our lives.

"If... Then..." Strategies

We all have emotional needs which must be acknowledged and met. The key is to remember while it is valid for us to fulfil our emotional needs, we don't have to use food to do so.

At times we can end up eating for emotional reasons rather than from any hunger or desire for nourishment. Sometimes we use food in an attempt to mask feelings we don't like to experience such as boredom, anger or sadness. These emotional eating habits can become ingrained over time but can also be reset.

The good news is there are many ways we can make ourselves feel good that don't involve extra unwanted calories. These could include phoning a friend, going for a walk, taking a bath, exercising or writing in a journal – just to name a few.

Dr Gordon Brune has identified the most common emotional states that trigger unhelpful and addictive behaviours such as emotional eating. He explains we are most susceptible to giving into temptations when we are bored, lonely, angry/anxious, stressed or tired, for which he has developed the acronym BLAST.

Being aware of your most common triggers in advance arms you for success, as you plan ahead and equip yourself with different strategies to meet those emotional needs.

Set yourself up with a list of "if.. then..." strategies for each of your triggers. These are strategies which you have thought of in advance and brainstormed as a variety of ways to boost your mood without the need for food.

For example:

- If I feel lonely... I will call my best friend.
- If I am bored... I will do a spring clean.
- If I get angry...I will jog around the block.
- If I feel stressed... I will take a hot bath.
- If I am tired... I will take a twenty minute power nap.

Other ideas could include:

If I am ...xyz... I will...

- ... do my favourite stretching routine.
- ... do 5 star jumps in every room of the house.
- ... pull funny faces in the mirror until I laugh.
- ... read something uplifting.
- ... have a herbal tea and read a magazine.
- ... listen to some upbeat music.
- ... plan my week ahead.
- ... de-clutter one drawer or cupboard.
- ... write a letter to a family member.
- ... head outside and take some photos.
- ... jot down three things I'm thankful for right now.
- ... watch a funny video.
- ... do some gardening.
- ... or any other ideas that will work best for you!

Make up your own specific list and put it up somewhere you will see it regularly as a visual reminder. Add a happy face or another positive image that speaks to you. This way you can easily refer to it and have a whole range of ideas to choose from at the exact moment you need them.

Always remember – there are lots of different ways to meet our emotional needs other than eating food!

Forward Casting

It is also good to know that temptations and cravings only last for between two to seven minutes. So if you can distract yourself for just a few minutes you can interrupt your train of thought and they will likely pass.

Another useful strategy when you are at the point of eating something unhelpful is to pause and ask yourself – "What food choice is going to leave me feeling the most satisfied in one to two hours' time?" – or even – "What can I do now that will leave me feeling at my best in one to two hours' time?" It may be that you don't need any food at all.

Use your willpower to make yourself pause for just a few seconds when you make the decision, and focus on what will give you the most long term satisfaction rather than giving in to instant gratification. This builds self-discipline over time.

Common Dysfunctional Thoughts

Every action we take is preceded by a thought. Once we can identify our thinking patterns and the types of thoughts that typically trip us up, we can choose to replace them with more useful thoughts. In her book *The Beck Diet Solution* psychologist Dr Judith Beck shares the following nine categories of dysfunctional thinking which help us identify the common thoughts to watch out for.

All or Nothing Thinking

I've just eaten badly, so I may as well give up eating well for the whole day.

Negative Fortune Telling

If I don't eat it now I'll end up eating it later any way.

Overly Positive Fortune Telling

I'll only eat a handful of potato chips, then I'll stop.

I can have a second helping, I'll make up for it later.

Emotional Reasoning

Since I feel like a failure for overeating, I must be a failure.

Mind Reading

They will think I'm rude if I turn down their baking.

Everyone will expect me to have another helping so I may as well.

Self-Deluding Thoughts

It won't count if no-one sees me while I'm eating or if I eat while walking around.

Unhelpful Rules

I can't waste food, I must finish everything on my plate.

Justification

I'm on holiday so it's ok for me to overeat.

I can't miss out on this because it's free.

Exaggerated Thinking

I can't help but give into my cravings.

The key is to be able to *recognise* and *replace* the common thought patterns you tend to have. For each of your most common dysfunctional thoughts, write down an alternative thought that will help you make a better choice.

For example: "My cravings are so strong, I can't resist them" could become "I know that my cravings ebb and flow, so if I distract myself now they will be less strong later."

"I can't waste food" could become "I can choose to discard this food rather than overeat if I want to, which will assist me in achieving my goals." If you have had it ingrained not to waste money, a good question to ask yourself is "How much is this rice/potato/bread actually worth?" – often it is only a few cents.

"I've had a bad day so it's ok to overeat" could become "It is healthy for me to want to relax and give myself comfort after a bad day and there are many ways I could do this, including ways that support my health."

Take some time to identify any of these common thoughts you may have had in the past. Write out new thought patterns to adopt. Again, having a visual reminder is powerful, so you might like to put your new thought patterns up on the wall where you will see them regularly.

Externalising

Another technique, when you're about to make a poor eating decision, is to externalise yourself and picture what your best self would say to your real self in that very moment. If you experience cravings and temptation, imagine you are standing beside yourself, looking at this person that you love. What advice would you give them?

Often poor eating choices are tied in with unhelpful self-talk. Rather than allowing negative self-talk to continue, interrupt it by being kind to yourself, speaking to yourself as you would to someone you love deeply. This "external view" technique is highly effective to interrupt a habitual behaviour that you'd like to change.

Practise being able to change course and congratulate yourself every time you do. This builds self-esteem which in turn helps you progress. Through repetition you can embed these new habits and achieve anything you truly desire!

Eat Fruit First

But you say, "I know I'm going to crave chocolate".

A practical tip to reset your sweet cravings is to "eat fruit first". This simple rule is one you can follow for a short time, using your willpower, until it becomes second nature. "Eat fruit first" doesn't mean that you have to avoid the treat that you crave altogether, but it allows you to have a more nutritional choice first.

So if the chocolate in your cupboard is calling out to you, have a nice juicy apple first (or some other yummy nutritious snack) then wait ten minutes and see if you still really want the chocolate. If you do, then have some. Just make sure you sit down to savour every bit.

Note it doesn't have to be fruit. I just find "eat fruit first" is a catchy saying to keep in mind. The same thing can be done for savoury cravings too by opting for some juicy carrot sticks with hummus or another good food choice as a first option.

This way you are much more likely to stop after the nutritious snack, which will be able to satisfy any real hunger or thirst and combat low blood sugar levels. Even if you do still have the treat food, it's not on an empty stomach and at least you have had something really nutritious first. If you can keep this up consistently for about six weeks you will most likely reset your cravings altogether!

Sunlight and Cravings

Another less well-known factor behind cravings is sun exposure. Sunlight affects cravings because of its role in regulating the hormones, serotonin and melatonin. Serotonin makes us feel happy and content with the world while melatonin helps us go to sleep and stay asleep throughout the night. These two hormones are always in an inverse relationship, meaning when one is high the other is low.

If we don't boost our serotonin levels, especially on first waking in the morning, we can feel tired and low for no apparent reason. As serotonin helps us to feel calm, relaxed and happy, when it drops we can feel like we just need a little something to give us a boost. We also instinctively know that carbohydrate rich foods help to boost serotonin. So before we know it we can be halfway through an unplanned and unneeded snack, which in turn causes blood sugar levels to spike and then dip, leaving us feeling even more tired and low!

If you tend to have cravings in the afternoon or evenings, boosting your serotonin levels may help eliminate them.

Get outdoors into daylight as soon as you get up. A ten minute walk around the block is ideal to set you up for a great day as the sunlight causes the serotonin level to rise and diminishes the melatonin. This works even on an overcast day. If leaving home is impractical for you, try eating breakfast outdoors; your back doorstep is fine. At the very least, throw back the curtains and spend some time by the window looking at the sky to let your body know a new day has started.

Sunlight has amazing effects on your mood and overall wellbeing. Adequate sunlight is essential to ensure optimal sleep, so it is important to spend time outdoors regularly throughout the day to help regulate your internal body clock and assist a more restorative deep sleep at night.

The Effects of Stress

Stress is more prevalent in our ever-busy modern lifestyles. Despite having so many time saving devices, supposedly giving us more free time, we have simply sped life up, fitting more in, rather than enjoying an improved quality of life.

While a certain level of stress is beneficial as it motivates us to get things done, ongoing (chronic) stress has a range of negative health consequences. Chronic stress affects us in many ways, including reduced immunity, poor digestion, weight gain and low mood. It also increases our likelihood of heart disease, high blood pressure, stroke and metabolic syndrome.

Fight or flight is the body's response to a perceived threat or danger. It causes certain hormones like adrenalin and cortisol to be released, speeds the heart rate, slows digestion, shunts blood to major muscle groups, and gives the body a temporary burst of energy and strength. When the perceived threat is gone, systems are designed to return to normal function via the relaxation response. But in times of chronic stress this doesn't happen often enough, causing damage to the body.

Whether we're stressed because of constant, heavy demands at work or we really are in danger, our bodies respond in the same way and prepare us to fight for our lives or run like crazy. Remaining in this fight or flight mode for a prolonged amount of time due to ongoing stress puts your health at risk.

Chronic stress contributes to weight gain because high cortisol levels slow metabolism, increase cravings for fatty, salty and sugary foods, alter blood sugar levels and cause mood swings and fatigue. Excessive stress even affects where we store fat, leading to increased abdominal fat storage and greater health risks.

This can lead to a vicious cycle where we constantly rush and feel overloaded. Rather than taking time to prepare and eat a wholesome meal to nourish ourselves, we can put even more stress on the body by eating processed food that fails to give us the nutrients our body needs.

So what do we do?

As well as making it a priority to nourish yourself with real food to help combat stress at a cellular level, it is essential to include routines in your day which engage the relaxation response. The number one way to do this is by breathing diaphragmatically. Breathing is the only part of the body's autonomic nervous system you can influence (as opposed to hair and nail growth, for example).

Deep full breaths signal to your body you are feeling calm which initiates your body's relaxation response. Daily rituals such as journaling, meditation, reading, listening to calming music and having a salt bath are also beneficial.

As well as this, your perception of what you have to do for the day and the expectations you put on yourself are important to re-assess. Stress can become a mindset but you can break it if you pay attention to your attitude.

Do you tense your shoulders and frown just thinking about your to do list, or do you say to yourself "I am just going to do the best I can today with the time that I have?"

It is incredibly important to pause, take a step back and reassess your expectations and the pressure you put on yourself.

> *Let go of trying to fit more than is physically possible into your day.*

Identify what is urgent and what is important and allow yourself to drop some of the urgent yet unimportant commitments that tend to get you off track.

Take note of thoughts you have about what you "should" do. We all have the same 24 hours to work with. Feeling busy is a perception in relation to how much we feel we should do. Any time you think to yourself "I really should do xyz" remember it is simply a self-imposed pressure. The freeing thing is that you can choose to let go.

Choose your priorities in life; focus on fitting those things into your daily routines first and release yourself from the pressure of everything else. Saying "no" to things can be your best time management strategy. Reply with a polite "no" if something does not jump out as a huge "yes" for you. It will lift a weight off your shoulders and it can quite literally lift a weight off your entire body if you have been experiencing stress-induced weight gain.

Great Digestion

Great digestion is central to everything that happens in your body and is especially important to get you feeling healthy and vital. Poor digestion can leave you feeling bloated, uncomfortable and lethargic.

Great health requires optimal digestion, absorption, and assimilation of food. However the prevalence of irritable bowel syndrome, food intolerances, leaky gut and other digestive problems is rapidly increasing along with our fast-paced lives. We need to *slow down!* Constant rushing and never ending to-do lists have a huge impact on our health as we can't digest well when in constant fight or flight mode.

Slowing down may sound simple to do, but as with so many things in life, being simple does not always equal being easy. As with all habit change, you need to recognise the need and be intentional to make the new habits a part of your life. If you are a busy, driven person you may need to add "be present and just breathe" to your already long to-do list, (preferably at the top!) Doing so will make such a difference to how you feel and allow you to thrive and achieve so much more.

The digestion process starts in your mouth, so mindful eating is the first step. We need to chew food well and allow the salivary enzymes to begin the digestion process. This is one of the simplest practical steps you can take, which can enhance your digestion so much it literally transforms how you feel (especially if you ever feel heavy, bloated or lethargic after meals).

For optimal digestion ensure you always

- sit in a relaxed setting to eat
- focus only on eating
- chew each mouthful 20 times
- pause occasionally during your meal
- eat to feel just satisfied not over-full
- sit and relax for 5-10 minutes after your meal.

Stomach acidity is the next key. We need a good level of hydrochloric acid to break food down before it passes into our intestines. The cooking aromas we smell while preparing a meal increase our stomach acidity in anticipation of eating. This natural process is missed when eating pre-packaged meals on the run. Drinking too much before or with meals also dilutes stomach acidity.

Practical suggestions to improve stomach acidity:

- Avoid drinking during meals. While water is incredibly important, aim to drink it between meals and minimise drinking 20-30 minutes either side of mealtimes.
- Try drinking one teaspoon of raw apple cider vinegar mixed with ¼ cup of water before meals. It is loaded with enzymes and creates a nice acid environment for good digestion. You can reduce the water over time and have just the apple cider vinegar. Some people prefer lemon juice. Experiment, being mindful of how you feel and see what works best for you.
- Enzyme-rich foods such as raw milk and cheese and tropical fruits like bananas, pineapple and papaya can also aid digestion.

We have over 400 different kinds of bacteria and yeasts in our gut and need the good bacteria to be winning the battle for us. An imbalance in digestive bacteria can lead to weight gain, acid reflux, chronic sickness, auto-immune disorders, hormonal imbalances, sinus infections and depression.

Practical suggestions to improve gut bacteria:

- Avoid highly-processed, sugar-laden foods that disrupt good digestion and feed nasty yeasts and bacteria in our gut.
- Boost your positive gut bacteria with a good probiotic or a quality yoghurt with active cultures.

If you have tried all of the above and are still having digestive discomfort then arrange for food sensitivity screening or find a trained practitioner to supervise an elimination diet, isolating the body's reaction to any offending foods.

Balancing Portions

Some of the most common questions I am asked about nutrition are around appropriate portion sizes. So here is a guide to help keep your portions in balance.

The best way to describe good meal portions is to use the guide that God gave you in the palm of your hands. Your hands are the perfect visual reminder each time you serve up your plate and they are personally tailored to you.

Your closed fist is approximately the size of your stomach when empty. Take a look at it and think about that for a moment.

Vegetables – If you hold your palms up together, open in front of you, and picture both hands full of a mixture of green and brightly coloured vegetables, this is what you want to aim for at each meal. Having at least half of your plate filled with vegetables is one of the best things you can do for your health. They don't have to all be on the same plate at the same time; this is where a salad entrée comes in handy to boost your vegetable intake.

Protein – The size and thickness of the palm of your hand, excluding fingers, represents the amount of good quality protein to include in your meal.

Carbohydrates – One hand is also excellent to determine the amount of complex carbohydrates you serve up. On a less active day aim for an amount the size and thickness of your palm, or if you've been highly active include your palm and fingers.

Extras – make two circles with each thumb and fore finger. This is a good way to think of extra fats and sauces you may wish to add to your meal.

This gives you a basic framework to help you manage portions. Just remember there are a wide range of factors that influence what your portions should be, such as how active you are, how much lean muscle tone you have, your total body mass and of course your goals.

Furthermore, it is challenging to break food down and truly classify it into the specific macronutrient groups of fats, carbohydrates and proteins, because virtually all foods have a combination of each macronutrient.

As a rough guide, sources of protein include foods such as eggs, meat, chicken, fish, legumes, beans and quinoa (although the latter three are relatively high sources of carbohydrate as well). Sources of fats include olive oil, avocado, coconut, butter, nuts and seeds. Sources of carbohydrate include root vegetables, brown rice, wholemeal pasta, wraps and bread (although some can be a relatively high source of protein too).

Without trying to break the macronutrients down further or overly complicate things, these simple guidelines based on your palms serve as a good visual reminder and one that you always carry with you.

For example when you're at your next barbecue, you can bear in mind it will be best to fill up on lots of delicious fresh salads, and just choose one appropriate piece of steak, or a few kebabs, rather than piling your plate with multiple pieces of meat that together well exceed the size of your palm.

Hunger and Satiety

There is a part of the brain called the satiety centre (located in the hypothalamus) that controls how satisfied we feel. You may already know it can take up to 20 minutes from when we start a meal for our brain to register that we are full and to remind us to stop eating.

High fibre real foods that take time and effort to chew, assist in boosting satiety. The chewing process sends messages from the muscles in your jaw to your satiety centre signalling that you may be getting full soon.

Including protein in meals increases satiety, as protein signals the brain to release appetite-suppressing hormones, shutting down the "feed me" cues sooner. Fats also add the satisfaction factor to meals as they delay the stomach emptying, so you feel fuller for longer.

To keep you feeling satisfied it is useful to pair proteins and fats together with carbohydrates in each of your meals and snacks. For example:

- Have a handful of raw nuts with a piece of fruit rather than a piece of fruit on its own.
- Have peanut butter on celery logs for a more satisfying snack than just the celery.
- Add some chicken and a vinaigrette to your salad wrap to make a rounded meal of it.

Most of all, consider how much you eat because of hunger and how much out of habit. Aim to get in touch with your hunger cues and wait until you are hungry before sitting down to a meal. Aim to feel satisfied not bloated after meals and have mild hunger sensations as the next meal time approaches.

If you wish to reduce your portion sizes, these quick tips may help:

- Always sit down to eat without distractions.
- Trial for a few days writing down what you are going to eat before eating it. This can be helpful for a short period of time to raise awareness.
- Use smaller serving plates. A full side plate is more appealing than a half empty larger plate.
- Plate meals up rather than putting everything on the table and keep leftovers out of reach.
- Sit down at the dinner table as a family and discuss your day.
- Mentally cut your plate in half and half again as you eat.
- Focus on enjoying the texture, flavours and aromas of food.
- Wait ten minutes after your first serve of a meal before you decide if you will have more.
- Set leftovers aside for the next day before sitting down to eat.
- Use thinly sliced sandwich bread rather than toast bread.
- Serve dessert in small ramekins or cups.
- Eat dessert and breakfast with a teaspoon.
- Cut treats or snacks in half and put the rest away.
- Use small plastic containers or re-sealable plastic bags to set out portions of snack foods rather than having the whole packet on hand.
- Avoid snacking while cooking (only break this rule with raw vegetables).
- Eat smaller meals more frequently.
- Brush your teeth straight after dinner to avoid evening snacking.
- Add flat or sparkling water to juice and other drinks to dilute them.
- Alternate other drinks with a glass of water.

– PART II –

Why Real Food

Food Processing

Food Labels

Preservatives and Additives

Antioxidants

The Beauty of Real Food

Food Processing

Most foods that are available to us have gone through some form of processing. Note that while I use the words "processed food" in a negative manner, it is important to bear in mind that not all processing is harmful or hugely detrimental. For example freezing preserves most of the nutrients in food. Traditionally fermented and cultured foods increase enzyme activity making their nutrients more readily available. Dehydrating foods preserves them, concentrates their flavour and can enhance their nutrients. Canned foods tend to be processed at the height of ripeness and the canning process can increase the absorption of antioxidants such as lycopene in tomatoes and reduce phytates in legumes, improving digestion.

On the other hand hydrogenated oils that have been heated to high temperatures create a by-product called trans fats which should be avoided. Grains such as wheat and rice are commonly milled multiple times to remove not only the husk but also the bran, germ and aleurone leaving only the endosperm, meaning that 90% of the original nutrients are lost. It is important to opt for wholegrains such as brown rice and wholemeal flour which retain those nutrients as well as fibre which improves satiety, aids digestion and reduces blood sugar spiking.

For foods to have a long shelf life, most need a mixture of additives and preservatives added to them. It is a good idea to understand more about what is in the food you buy which starts with understanding the food labels.

Food Labels

The first place to start on a food label is the ingredients list. Avoid products with overly long ingredient lists containing a lot of unpronounceable words and numbers. Look for products that have short ingredient lists with natural, identifiable items. For example you can buy a peanut butter which contains 100% roasted peanuts, or you can buy one with a long list of ingredients including sugar, salt and emulsifiers. In the next section I explain more about additives and preservatives to watch out for.

Labels always list ingredients in order of their quantity, starting with the largest. You may find salt and sugar often sneak up into one of the first three ingredients on a list. You can, however, find many products containing just one item on their ingredient list. This way you know exactly what you are getting. Beware of items such as crackers or bread that appear to be wholemeal but which contain wheat flour, often before whole wheat flour in the ingredients list. This means they are made up of a majority of refined white flour.

Alongside the ingredients list, you may want to look at the nutritional panel which gives you a breakdown of the macronutrients within the food. This can be useful at times to compare similar products.

It is best to use the per 100g column. This keeps it simple and means you can compare any products quickly and easily even if they have different serving sizes. This also allows you to think of what you're eating in terms of a percentage. You might be surprised to learn that your breakfast cereal is over 33% sugar for example. Many of them are.

When you look at the per 100g column, the number of grams listed always equals the percentage of whatever it is in the product.

For example:

8 grams of protein = 8% protein,

9 grams of fibre = 9% fibre,

15 grams of fat = 15% fat, and so on.

Note that some categories are broken right down and listed as part of the total e.g. fats and carbohydrates are often separated out; just be aware that you don't need to add these numbers together as they are part of the total above.

Fat	26g
- Saturated Fat	4g
- Trans Fat	1g
Carbohydrates	32g
- Sugar	12g

For example in the product above there are 26 grams total fat of which 4 grams are saturated fat, 1 gram is trans fat and the remaining 21 grams must be unsaturated. Similarly, the total carbohydrates are 32 grams with 12 grams of sugar meaning that the remaining 20 grams are complex carbohydrates.

There are no set ranges to aim for as different foods will have completely different nutritional profiles. What can be useful however is to compare two identical foods or products from different brands with one another. When comparing two similar products it is generally best to opt for foods with less

- fat
- sugar
- salt

and those with higher

- protein
- dietary fibre.

Just bear in mind that individual macronutrients don't tell the whole picture. The list of ingredients is the best place to start.

Watch out for bold claims on the front of the packet proclaiming health benefits. These always emphasise one aspect of a product; for example that it is low-fat without pointing out that it is high sugar, or that it is sugar free without pointing out that it uses artificial sweeteners. Remember that the healthiest foods usually have no health marketing labels whatsoever. Have you ever seen an apple or a carrot with health claims?

Preservatives and Additives

Processed convenience foods rely on preservatives to extend their shelf life. Their role is to prevent bacteria, yeast and mould growth, preserve colour and keep food from going bad.

It can be challenging to avoid preservatives altogether as they can be found in almost any type of food or drink. While most have been deemed at safe levels in the quantities they are found in any given food, it is suggested that cumulatively if too many are eaten on a regular basis, they can cause harm over the long term.

While a healthy body is able to produce the enzymes required to neutralise many of these substances, if it is overloaded with junk food it may not be able to cope and poor health will result. So, minimising exposure is essential for optimal health.

These are some of the most common ones to avoid:

Potassium Sorbate (food additive number 202) found in cheese, dairy products, yoghurt, wine, dried meat, pickles, apple cider and dips. It is used to prevent mould growth and is reported to cause DNA damage.

Sodium Benzoate (211) is used in carbonated drinks, oral medications, mouth washes and added to acidic foods such as pickles, fish and oyster sauces, salad dressings, jams and fruit juices to enhance their flavour. It works by increasing the acidity of the food. When mixed with vitamin C, sodium benzoate forms benzene, a known carcinogen. Studies have shown that it may increase hyperactive behaviour in some children.

Sulphur Dioxide (220) and **Sulphites** (221-228) are used to preserve the flavour and colour in fruits, dried fruits, vinegar, juices, cordials, soft drinks, sauces, beers and wines. Sulphites release sulphur dioxide, inhibit bacterial growth, reduce spoilage and prevent the browning of fresh food. Sulphites can cause allergy and hay fever like reactions, wheezing in asthmatics and hives.

Sodium Nitrate (250) and **Sodium Nitrite** (251) are used in processed meat such as bacon, ham, sausages, hot dogs, luncheon meats and cured meats to preserve the meat, enhance colour and inhibit the growth of bacteria. When used for curing, nitrates react with the meat tissues to form nitrites. Nitrites can combine with chemicals in the stomach to form nitrosamine — a carcinogen found in cigarettes. Food safety organisations restrict food manufacturers from putting these preservatives in baby foods but not on foods typically consumed by many children such as sausages and luncheon meat.

Propionates (280-283) are commonly used to prevent mould growth in bread and bakery products. They are also permitted in cheese, fruit and vegetable products. Reported side effects include migraine, headaches, stomach upsets, skin rashes, nasal congestion, depression, tiredness, irritability and restlessness.

Potassium Bromate is used to increase volume in flour and breads. It has been shown to cause cancer in animal test subjects. Small amounts can pose risks for people.

Butylated Hydroxyanisole (BHA) and **Butylated Hydroxytoluene** (BHT) are used as preserving agents in cereals and potato chips. They stop the fats and oils in foods from turning rancid. Studies have shown that these preservatives lead to hyperactivity, angioedema, asthma, rhinitis, dermatitis, tumours and they can affect oestrogen balance and levels.

It is also important to avoid additives such as:

Trans Fats which are found in Hydrogenated and Partially Hydrogenated Oils such as palm oil and soybean oil. These oils contain high levels of trans fats, which raise bad cholesterol and lower good cholesterol, contributing to risk of heart disease.

Artificial Sweeteners are found in diet and sugar free products. These can negatively affect metabolism, increase sweet and sugar cravings and some have been linked to cancer, headaches, dizziness, anxiety and hallucinations.

High Fructose Corn Syrup (HFCS) is found in many processed baked goods. HFCS is not easily metabolised by the liver and is more likely to lead to excess fat storage. It increases risk for type II diabetes, coronary heart disease, stroke and cancer. Any food containing HFCS is a sure sign that it is a highly processed food to be avoided.

Monosodium Glutamate is found in salad dressing, chips, noodles and frozen meals. It stimulates appetite and can cause headaches, nausea, weakness, wheezing, change in heart rate, burning sensations and difficulty in breathing. It can be hard to spot as it is sometimes included under the label "flavourings", "natural flavours" or "seasonings". Look out for all glutamates which are labelled 621-625.

Antioxidants

Antioxidants are important chemicals that occur naturally in a range of foods. They help protect your body against cancer, heart disease and the effects of ageing. They fight free radicals in the body that come about through exposure to pollution, chemicals, stress and sun damage. Free radicals can cause damage and inflammation to body tissue so we need a good amount of antioxidants to keep us in good health for the long term. Real whole foods are fantastic sources of key antioxidants such as beta-carotene, lycopene, lutein, anthocyanins, vitamin C, vitamin E, folate and selenium.

Beta-Carotene creates the red and orange pigments in several fruits and vegetables. The body converts them into vitamin A which is essential for good eyesight and eye health as well as boosting immunity. Good sources include golden kumara (sweet potato), carrots, pumpkin (squash), broccoli, kale, spinach, peas, mangoes, rock melon and apricots.

Lycopene gives many fruit and vegetables their red colour. It prevents cell damages and is a known preventative against prostate cancer. Research shows processed forms of tomatoes such as diced tomatoes and tomato paste allow lycopene to be more readily absorbed by the body, so they are an especially good source to consume. Other sources include watermelons, guavas, papayas, apricots, pink grapefruits, cooked red capsicums (bell peppers), asparagus and purple cabbage.

Lutein is the pigment found in dark leafy green vegetables and in eggs. It supports good eye health and is known to prevent eye diseases including age-related macular degeneration and cataracts. Good sources include broccoli, silver beet (Swiss chard), spinach, kale, courgette (zucchini) and eggs.

Anthocyanins are flavonoids that make certain fruits and vegetables vivid red to blue. They are proven to reduce inflammation, to help prevent cancer, cardiovascular disease and diabetes. Good sources include blackberries, blueberries, black currants, grapes, plums, cherries, eggplant (aubergine), broccoli, red cabbage, black beans, kidney beans and even banana.

Vitamin C is essential to form collagen to repair and rebuild body tissue such gums, bones, teeth and blood vessels. It also supports the immune system and helps with iron absorption. Good sources include kiwifruit, capsicum (bell pepper), citrus fruits, strawberries, tomatoes, dark leafy green vegetables and broccoli.

Vitamin E is important for immune function and for the protection of cell membranes. Good sources include avocado, almonds, sunflower seeds, walnuts, peanut butter, spinach, broccoli, olive oil, shrimp and tofu.

Folate is important prior to and during pregnancy for healthy foetus development. It is also reported to combat osteoporosis, cervical cancer and heart disease and it acts as an anti-depressant by releasing serotonin. Good sources include beans, lentils, leafy greens, avocado, asparagus, broccoli and fortified cereals and breads.

Selenium is an antioxidant mineral that works together with other antioxidants such as vitamins C and E. It supports immune system function, thyroid function and fertility in men. Good sources include Brazil nuts, sunflower seeds, fish, shellfish, meat, poultry, eggs, onions, brown rice, whole wheat bread and oats.

The Beauty of Real Food

Rarely have I met a woman who did not take an interest in her appearance. Women of all ages desire to look and feel beautiful, it's just part of human nature. While it is not the most important thing, it does contribute to how we feel and how we go about life. What we eat absolutely underpins how we look as well as how we feel.

I love the top four tips for beautiful skin from national award winning New Zealand beauty therapist Pania Ryan, which are to:

1. Drink lots of water.
2. Eat a range of nutritious whole foods.
3. Exercise regularly.
4. Wear a good sunscreen every day.

These four points are the basis of your beauty routine. First and foremost you must get good stuff into your body to allow it to repair and replenish itself.

Skin is the body's largest organ. It makes sense that what is good for your whole body is good for your skin. The wonderful nutrients in food lead to plump, glowing skin, an even skin tone, shiny strong hair, bright eyes and an overall vibrancy. Plus they can boost your mood to make you smile more which is always a most beautiful thing!

More importantly, our health is determined by what we eat and how well we digest and absorb the nutrients that foods contain. Our food can either boost or diminish our immunity, our energy levels and our overall sense of wellbeing.

Here is an overview of some of the most important food groups to consume for optimal health and beauty. Make sure you get a good quantity, quality and variety of these into your diet every week to look and feel amazing.

Colourful Fruit and Vegetables

Orange-red fruit and vegetables such as carrots, kumara, capsicum (bell pepper), apricots, melon, and mangoes are full of beta-carotene which is converted to vitamin A in your body. Beta-carotene acts as an antioxidant, preventing cell damage and promoting good eye health.

Citrus fruits, kiwifruit and berries are high in vitamin C. They provide you important fibre, folate and potassium. Vitamin C not only boosts your immunity. It is also a key skin-care ingredient and a powerful antioxidant that helps maintain smooth taut skin by preventing premature ageing due to free radicals. It helps your body produce collagen, which helps prevent wrinkles and keeps your gums in good health. Strawberries, raspberries and blackberries have high levels of ellagic acid which increases skin's ability to hold moisture.

Purple fruits and vegetables such as plums, blueberries, blackberries, cherries, red grapes, red cabbage, eggplant, and beetroot (beets), contain high concentrations of the antioxidant anthocyanins which reduce inflammation.

White vegetables such as potatoes, parsnips, cauliflower and mushrooms contain important nutrients including potassium, magnesium and vitamin C. Garlic and onions have anti-inflammatory and immunity boosting properties as well as adding a great base of flavour to a wide range of meals.

Green vegetables are essential to support a great number of processes in your body. They help with purifying blood, strengthening your immune system, and promoting healthy gut, liver and kidney function. Dark leafy green vegetables in particular, like spinach, rocket, kale and silver beet (Swiss chard) are packed full of calcium, iron, zinc, vitamins A, C and K, chlorophyll and folate. They help your skin produce more fresh new cells and get rid of the old ones, reducing dryness and keeping your face looking bright and young.

To ensure proper absorption of carotenoids and fat soluble vitamins (A, D, E and K) it is important to consume some fat along with the vegetables that supply these. For example add some avocado, olives or extra virgin olive oil to your salad which are all high in healthy monounsaturated fat.

In addition, whole fruit and vegetables are low calorie and high fibre, making you feel full and satisfied. They are nature's wonderful balanced nutritional package. Most are low Glycaemic Index (GI) meaning they give you a steady balanced energy release that won't spike your blood sugar levels leaving you tired, hungry and craving food again soon after.

They help you avoid overeating which can make you feel heavy and lethargic and leads to excess body fat.

In short vegetables are incredible! I can't stress enough the importance of eating a great variety and amount of delicious fruits and vegetables. Aim to eat the rainbow by consuming a mixture of reds, oranges, yellows, whites, greens, blues and purples throughout the week.

Fish and Seafood

Two key nutrients in fish and seafood are omega-3 fatty acids and zinc

Omega-3s are essential fatty acids not made in the body, so you must get them from your diet. Fish such as salmon, sardines, anchovies, mackerel, trout and tuna provide EPA and DHA omega-3s. ALA a plant based omega-3 fatty acid, is found in walnuts, flaxseeds (also called linseeds) and olive oil. It is best to get omega-3s from whole foods if possible, however supplements may be beneficial if required. Aim to eat fish high in DHA and EPA omega-3s two times a week and include seeds and vegetable oils in small amounts most days.

Omega-3s are anti-inflammatory, reduce redness and dryness and slow down the skin's ageing process. They contribute to keeping your skin moist, supple and your hair shiny and in good condition.

Omega-3s not only improve appearance but are essential for proper body function and deliver a range of great health benefits. They can assist sufferers of arthritis, asthma and ADHD; enhance circulation, and are an important natural defence against depression. They are also important during pregnancy for the neurological development of the baby. Some research also suggests omega-3s may help protect against Alzheimer's disease and dementia.

Zinc assists in the production of new cells giving you glowing skin. It protects your cell membranes, helps maintain collagen and keeps your skin clear due to its role in metabolising testosterone which affects the production of sebum, an oily substance that is a primary cause of acne. Zinc also improves your immune function and supports thyroid and adrenal glands.

Excellent sources of zinc are oysters, crab, and lobster. Non-seafood sources include spinach, pumpkin seeds (pepitas), flaxseed oil, sunflower seeds, chia seeds, walnuts, cashews, beef and lamb.

Raw Nuts and Seeds

Nuts and seeds contain healthy fats that support optimal body function, mood and appearance. As well as being full of flavour and useful for adding texture to a meal they are a natural anti-depressant giving you even more reason to be happy when you eat them. Nuts are an important source of vitamin E, another antioxidant good at protecting the skin from sun damage. A small handful of raw nuts, such as almonds, walnuts, cashews or Brazil nuts, is great to include in your diet each day.

You might also like to spend a little more to get pine nuts, pecans and macadamias from time to time. Just two Brazil nuts as a morning snack, for example, will meet your required selenium intake for the day. Note that nuts are energy dense so just a few will do. You can also use ground almond meal or LSA (ground linseeds, sunflower seeds and almonds) in baking or add them to breakfast cereals. These are both a great gluten free option to replace flour for those that have coeliac disease or are gluten intolerant.

Seeds are essentially kernels of life packed with high concentrations of a wide range of vitamins, minerals, proteins and essential oils.

Stock up on raw seeds such as pumpkin (pepitas), sunflower, sesame, chia and flaxseeds. Store them in airtight containers in a dark cool place to keep them at their best. They are delicious added to salads, in cereal, on top of yoghurt, in trail mix, blended into baking, as a garnish or simply on their own.

Pumpkin seeds (pepitas) are a skin superfood because of their high zinc levels and are packed with protein, vitamin B, magnesium, manganese, iron and copper. They can boost your mood and improve your sleep due to the important amino acid L-tryptophan, which is required for the body to produce serotonin, our happiness hormone.

Sunflower seeds contain vitamin E, magnesium and phytosterols which reduce cholesterol and improve immunity.

Sesame seeds are a rich source of calcium to build tooth enamel and strengthen bones. They provide you a good source of manganese, copper and a wide range of other minerals, vitamins and dietary fibre.

Chia seeds are often referred to as a superfood because of their high concentration of protein, fibre, calcium, magnesium, vitamin C, iron, and omega-3.

Flaxseeds are rich in the antioxidant ALA omega-3 and fibre. Just one tablespoon of flaxseeds contains as much fibre as half a cup of cooked oat bran. They are best consumed ground up (such as in LSA) so the body can absorb and use all the nutrients.

Activating nuts by soaking them is reported to increase their nutritional benefits. It makes them more easily digested by reducing the phytic acid that is naturally present, which can reduce nutrient absorption. You can soak nuts and use them straight away in cooking or dry them at a low temperature and store in airtight containers.

Similarly, soaking and sprouting seeds brings them to life and increases their nutritional value. Seeds naturally contain enzyme inhibitors, which keep them from going bad but which also make them difficult to digest. Once a seed is sprouted the enzyme inhibitors are deactivated, protein and enzymes are increased and the seed's nutrients become more readily available. See **pg 237** for a guide to soaking and sprouting.

Whole Grains

There are many different types of whole grains which contain fibre, protein, vitamins, minerals, phytonutrients, and antioxidants. Examples include: amaranth, brown rice, buckwheat, bulgur wheat, corn, einkorn wheat, emmer wheat, kamut wheat, millet, oatmeal, pearl barley, quinoa, spelt wheat, whole rye, whole wheat and wild rice.

In recent years carbohydrates, including whole grains, have been criticised as being unhealthy. However not all carbohydrates should be lumped together and labelled as bad.

Wheat flour (white flour) has had its bran and germ removed, meaning fibre, vitamins and minerals are lost and often need to be added back through a fortification process. Removing the bran and germ improves the shelf life of white flour but reduces its fibre and goodness overall. When rice is milled, the husks are removed, resulting in brown rice. This is then further polished at least three more times, removing the bran, germ and aleurone, resulting in white rice.

The challenge with products made from highly refined grains is their lack of fibre, protein and flavour which make them easy to overeat compared with whole grain alternatives. Consequently, many people over consume meals that are almost entirely made up of these highly processed foods (which often also include hydrogenated oils, salt, sugar and other additives.) The energy from these refined carbohydrates is quickly converted to glucose in the blood stream, especially if they are eaten with very little protein or fat to slow down this harmful glucose rush.

On the other hand, wholegrain foods contain the goodness of the entire grain including the bran and the germ along with its fibre, protein, iron and vitamins. They are lower Glycaemic Index, complex carbohydrate rich foods, meaning that they provide a slower steadier release of glucose into the blood stream, providing you with sustained energy. They engage the body's satiety response faster and help prevent blood sugar and insulin spiking, which commonly occurs with highly processed foods. Hence, whole grains reduce your risk of diabetes, heart attack and stroke.

Whole grains also improve skin complexion as they contain antioxidants such as rutin, bioton and selenium which prevent your skin becoming dry or scaly, promote elasticity and combat inflammation and environmental related skin damage.

Quinoa while not being a true grain, as it comes from the spinach and beetroot (beets) family, is worth mentioning here as it resembles grain in its everyday use. It is an energy sustaining low GI carbohydrate as well as a fantastic source of complete protein. This means it supplies the body with all of the essential amino acids required for repair.

Gluten is also worth a mention. Gluten is a protein found in wheat, barley and rye which is hard for some people to digest. This affects a minority of people including those with coeliac disease (estimated at 1-2% of the population) and those with wheat allergy or gluten sensitivity (estimated at 2-7% of the population).

It is interesting that we are seeing such an increase in gluten free products both in supermarkets and on restaurant and café menus. There is a misconception that gluten free equates to healthy. If you are diagnosed with coeliac disease or have confirmed a sensitivity (identified through blood testing or an elimination diet), then avoiding gluten is sensible.

In these cases, stick to gluten free whole grains such as quinoa, amaranth, buckwheat (which despite the name contains no wheat), corn, millet and brown rice. If however you are not gluten intolerant you can enjoy the full range of whole grains available.

Note that oats are sometimes referred to as low-gluten. They contain the avenin form of gluten which some people tolerate while others do not. Also, because they are often grown in close proximity to wheat, or processed in the same facilities, they can be cross-contaminated with gluten. If you have coeliac disease or an allergy to avenin you will need to avoid oats, but can enjoy rolled quinoa in their place.

Pulses

Pulses such as chickpeas (garbanzo beans), red, green and brown lentils, beans and peas are fantastic additions to any diet. They are rich in both fibre and protein, and have high levels of minerals and vitamins. They are anti-ageing because of the high levels of antioxidants they contain that reduce cell damage.

Not only are pulses tasty and versatile, they are inexpensive and incredibly filling which means that they make meals go a long way. They can complement or substitute for other protein options such as meat, poultry or fish. If you have meat lovers in your family try starting out by halving the meat content and adding lentils or chickpeas (garbanzo beans) to your typical curry, casserole or other meals.

Dried varieties of pulses simply need to be rinsed and soaked in advance of cooking, which is an easy practice once you get into the habit (and are a meal planning whizz!) Canned varieties are also available for convenience. They make great instant salads or are fantastic additions to soups, casseroles, curries, pies, oven bakes and stir fries as well as making hummus and can even be used in baking.

Meat and Poultry

Red meat such as beef, lamb and venison and poultry such as chicken and turkey, are all excellent sources of complete protein, containing the full range of amino acids required to build muscle and repair tissue. Maintaining lean body mass is important for healthy body function and to prevent excessive fat gain as muscle tone burns extra calories. Consuming adequate protein will also satisfy your hunger for a longer period after meals.

As a note for vegetarians, it is possible to attain adequate protein without eating meat. In particular we need to consume the nine essential amino acids which our body cannot produce. This can be achieved by consuming an adequate variety of protein rich foods such as quinoa, beans, legumes, peas, leafy greens, brown rice, whole grains, nuts and seeds.

Red meat is an especially good source of haem iron which is much more easily absorbed by the body than the non-haem form of iron found in plants. Iron helps form haemoglobin for oxygen transportation. Maintaining adequate iron levels is particularly important for women before and during pregnancy, as iron is vital for the growth and development of the foetal brain. Protein, iron and zinc all work to strengthen the immune system, assisting healing and producing antibodies that protect the body from infections.

Meat is a rich source of vitamin B12, which helps make DNA, repairs brain tissue and is vital for the proper functioning of nearly every system in your body. A lack of B12 can speed up ageing and lead to neurological disorders, mental illness, cancer, cardiovascular disease, and infertility.

Red meat has significantly more B12 (as well as more iron and zinc) than white meat. Unless you eat a lot of shellfish, red meat can be your best and easiest source of these vital nutrients.

Meat also provides other B vitamins, vitamin A and vitamin D. These promote good vision, stronger teeth and bones and also support the central nervous system which promotes mental health. The tryptophan and vitamin B5 in meat help to calm the body and combat stress. For people who lack sun exposure and don't eat a lot of oily fish, red meat can help prevent vitamin D deficiency.

Poultry is also rich in minerals such as phosphorus and calcium that help maintain strong bones, and selenium to reduce the risk of arthritis.

Another big benefit of eating meat is maintaining the health of your skin. Red meat protein has the highest concentration of the amino acids glycine and proline which, along with zinc, help produce collagen for smooth clear skin.

When shopping for meat, opt for quality cuts rather than highly processed products and prepare your own real food meals whenever possible. It is preferable to purchase smaller portions of high quality meat than to stock up on low-cost low-quality options which, in terms of your health, are really false economy. To stretch your budget, you will find many quality slow cook style cuts of red meat and whole chickens or poultry on the bone are less expensive options than steak or chicken breast. These make fantastic casseroles, roasts or slow cooker meals which can be incredibly healthy as well as budget friendly. The added benefit is being able to make your own homemade stock or bone broth as well.

If you do purchase any pre-made meat products, such as sausages, patties or packaged meals, check the labels and choose those with the least additives and highest meat and protein content. Once you are set up with my meal planning systems, you will have your own easy meals on hand in your home freezer, so you won't need to rely on any store bought ones at all.

Eggs

Eggs contain the full range of amino acids in the balanced proportion for your body, making them an excellent and complete source of protein. They have a high satiety rating keeping you feeling fuller for longer and reducing snacking. They contain all of the B vitamins, as well as Vitamins A, D and E and a wide range of minerals including iodine, phosphorous and selenium.

They can be a great start to the day if you prefer a cooked breakfast. They are quick and easy to prepare; whether boiled, scrambled, poached or cooked into frittatas or omelettes. They can also be added into baking and other meals.

Always opt for free-range eggs, which is a vote against cruelty to animals and gives you higher quality eggs because the laying hens' diet has huge influence on the nutritional content. Free-range eggs contain more vitamins and are higher in essential omega-3 fatty acids which are often deficient in our diets. Free-range eggs are excellent for the health of your brain and skin and improve blood lipid profiles.

Dairy Products

Dairy products can be a satisfying part of your diet and add a lot of flavour, as well as vital nutrients such as calcium, phosphorus, zinc, and vitamins A and B12. There has been a proliferation of low-fat and no-fat dairy products made available which contain high levels of sugar and/or artificial sweeteners. I recommend sticking to the original full fat versions which have less sugar or additives.

If you can find a good quality source you may consider opting for raw milk which is rich in nutrients. If you are lactose intolerant, there are several dairy free options such as almond milk, coconut milk, coconut cream or cashew cream.

Always opt for real butter rather than margarine or table spreads containing man-made trans fats. Out of all of the nutritional controversies, one of the few things everyone agrees on and which the studies also bear out, is the importance of avoiding trans fats. Keep butter in a butter dish at room temperature for easy spreading.

While we don't want to over indulge, small amounts of butter add great flavour to food. It can be used in moderate temperature cooking up to 175°C (350°F).

Greek yoghurt is a thick, creamy style of yoghurt high in protein and probiotics to improve digestion. Opt for a quality organic natural Greek yoghurt where possible. A lovely adaptation is to turn your yoghurt into Labneh which is like homemade cream cheese. (See **pg 196** to discover how easy this is).

Both of these are incredibly versatile and can be used in either sweet or savoury meals, in sauces, baking or just on their own or with a few berries or seeds as a snack.

If you need to wean yourself or family members off sweetened yoghurt, try serving Greek yoghurt with a natural sweetener such as honey or maple syrup and gradually reducing the amount over a couple of weeks. Taste buds change and adapt quickly!

Cheese is a flavoursome, protein rich food that helps make a meal more satisfying. Opt for real cheese which is made traditionally through a process of curdling and culturing milk. It should have a short ingredients' list including only; milk, salt, cultures and rennet. Avoid those with extra preservatives, colours and other additives.

As well as standard Edam cheese which is good for grating into a meal, I use different cheeses for a variety of flavour such as ricotta, feta, blue cheese and parmesan. Always opt for blocks of parmesan and shave or grind it fresh into your food rather than using the pre-ground versions which contain preservatives. You will be surprised at how long a block of fresh parmesan will last and what a difference it will make to your meal.

Hydration

Water, while not a food, is so vitally important to our health that I simply could not avoid mentioning it here. Water sustains life. It is essential for so many bodily functions and processes such as liver function, metabolising fat, rehydrating joints and of course skin complexion, plumping up our skin cells to reduce wrinkles, plus it even improves our posture, making us taller. Without adequate hydration our brains aren't able to function properly, leading to poor concentration, listlessness and irritability, which makes it even harder to make positive health choices.

There is much debate as to how much water we should drink. To keep it really simple (rather than trying to work out millilitres per kilo of body weight) the easiest way to stay well hydrated is to check the colour of your urine. When you go to the bathroom, aim to make the result long and clear.

Pale straw-coloured or clear urine indicates you have drunk enough water. Yellow urine means that you are dehydrated (unless of course you have taken some sort of supplement that can often make your urine bright yellow or orange). Remember that drinking water is a simple but incredibly effective way to boost your health, so it is worth checking.

Rather than having a vague goal to "drink more water", a much better way to stay hydrated is to add practical routines, rituals and visual reminders into your day to ensure you drink water regularly. These could include drinking two glasses of water upon waking, having a glass and a jug on your desk, filling and consuming a drink bottle of water twice a day or linking drinking to routine tasks such as sending a text message. In winter try out herbal (non-caffeinated) teas or hot water with a slice of lemon. If you do consume drinks containing sugar, caffeine or alcohol aim to at least alternate these with water on a one for one basis.

Often I am asked whether I recommend smoothies or juicing. These can be healthy practices, although remember that it is important to treat any drink containing calories as a meal or snack. In a lot of cases people will not mentally register a glass of juice in the same way as a meal, but would feel more satisfied eating the fruits and vegetables whole.

Making your own smoothies or juices can be beneficial, especially if it helps you get more green leafy vegetables into your day that you otherwise wouldn't consume. I prefer smoothies which include all of the fibre of the whole fruits and/or vegetables, whereas juicing removes and wastes much of this. If, however, you find it challenging to get enough green vegetables into your diet, fresh juicing can be beneficial if this is what you enjoy and if it is predominantly vegetable juice that you are consuming.

There is a common misconception that purchased fruit juices are healthy. Most, however, are sugar laden and again people often fail to register the extra calories they are consuming. Because fruit juice lacks the fibre of the original fruit it also causes more of a glucose rush which spikes blood sugar levels.

Bottom line, the best and most important thing to drink is water, and plenty of it.

– PART III –

Real Food Made Easy

Eleven Meal Planning Principles

Step by Step Menu Planning

Eleven Meal Planning Principles

Now that you are hopefully convinced of the plethora of reasons to eat real food and are armed with a whole range of ways to overcome emotional eating so you can relax and eat well...

let's make real food fuss-free for you!

I have developed the following principles to explain exactly how I make nutritious home cooking incredibly easy to do. When you understand the *why* behind something the next step is being equipped with the knowledge to make it happen. This chapter explains all of the practical *how to* steps to save you time and effort and make meal planning and preparation simple so you naturally boost your real food and feel fantastic.

I used to think these principles were commonplace and everyone must use them. Then it dawned on me that not everyone does. I kept fielding questions about how I find the time to eat well, juggle a young family and a business, all with a husband often away, and how we manage to do this within a budget. So here is my chance to answer these questions for you.

It is incredibly important to me that my family and I eat well. To ensure this I plan ahead, use shortcuts, make my meals flow, keep a well-stocked freezer and use lots of tips and tricks to boost flavour without compromising nourishment so that we always have nutritious home cooked meals.

In the past two years I can count the number of takeaways we've had on one hand as it's been so easy and delicious to eat in! I don't share that to boast, but simply to inspire you that you can easily do the same, if you so desire.

Trust me, I didn't always live like this.

As a young married couple my husband and I used to buy packet mixes and ready-made frozen food. Devilled sausages from a packet mix were pretty much the height of our culinary expertise. We had a bare spice cupboard, no herbs or garden vegetables and knew very little about food combinations, how to put a balanced meal together or how to use leftovers. Our dinner plans usually started as we walked in the door late after work when we would reach for raw meat from the freezer. Cooking was only ever a chore. I would occasionally think to myself that meal planning would be a nice idea but never became organised enough to give it a go.

You may be in the same boat as I was, or perhaps further down the track and already have a few of the following principles mastered – If so, good on you!

As with any system, the key to making this work is to understand and follow **all** the principles together. The power really is in the way these principles work in unison to make life super easy and smooth running for you. The only way to discover what a difference they make, is to try it out for yourself.

In brief, my eleven principles are to

1. Plan your week
2. Work your plan
3. Display your menu
4. Shop to your menu
5. Simplify your shopping
6. Batch cook by default
7. Set extra portions away first
8. Shortcut
9. Fresh is always first
10. Never waste food
11. Enjoy a weekly cook-up.

1. Plan your week

Plan your menu for each week in advance to suit your lifestyle. On the nights when you know you will be home late or have limited time, plan a quick and easy ten minute dinner, a meal that cooks itself or a "twice as nice" defrosted meal. (I'll explain how you set these up further on. It's an essential part of the system.)

Many years ago, when I first started meal planning I used a system that had a basic template for every week.

Ours went like this:

Theme	Examples
Mon – "Fabulous Fresh Fish"	Homemade gourmet fish and chips, pan fried fillets, oven baked fish, fish pie etc.
Tues – "Double Trouble"	Usually a lasagne, casserole, curry, pasta bake or pie that will freeze well, made in a double portion.
Wed – "Meat Lovers"	A "meat and three veg" kind of night, often chicken or beef either in a stir fry, kebabs, curry or on its own with the vegetables on the side.
Thur – "Twice as Nice"	Defrost a meal from the previous week – ahhh bliss!
Fri – "Friday Fun Night"	Pizza or a fun hands-on meal like wraps or French crepes.
Sat – "Easy Tea"	Eggs on toast, soup, baked beans, omelette etc.
Sun – "Family Roast"	Roast lamb, beef, chicken etc. A great meal to share with friends and for lunch leftovers during the week!

This was brilliant as an ideas starter. Having this template made it so much easier to come up with a balanced variety of meals throughout the week. I was of course flexible with it all and often switched nights around. The easy tea night would just be skipped if we were out socialising on a Saturday. If we were entertaining we could swap in the roast for any other meal.

I have long since lost the piece of paper on which I wrote out this list of fun names for each night. I no longer use this method, but it was the starting point from which my meal planning system evolved. I have now moved away from this fixed structure to allow my meals to flow more around the produce that is seasonal, available or on special.

The biggest change however is that I highly recommend double, triple or quadruple batch cooking at every opportunity, which keeps life super simple and allows you to easily maintain a library of meals in your freezer. I also aim to make every meal flow onto the next lunch or dinner, or to become a key ingredient for a future meal. I love having three, four or five nights off cooking every single week by making my freezer work for me.

Picture not having to cook half the time!
Sounds great, don't you think?

After these eleven principles I walk you through a detailed step by step guide to creating the perfect meal plan to suit your week.

2. Work your plan

My military husband often reminds me that no plan, no matter how good, will ever be carried out to the letter. So while step one is all about having a plan, which gives you focus, working your plan is all about being able to adapt as the week evolves. Be flexible and change the menu as events crop up or if meals don't turn out quite as anticipated.

You might have unexpected guests for dinner or be invited out at the last minute. You may come down with an illness or have to deal with an emergency. This is real life.

Often people avoid meal planning from a fear that they might waste food if their plans change. I will explain not only how to save time and money by meal planning the way I do, but also how best to store leftovers, and how to thaw and reheat meals in a way that gives them appeal – often things taste even better the second time around. This way you never waste a thing and can jump at the chance of a night out without worrying about having to stick to the plan.

As you become more practised and confident with meal planning you will be able to easily adapt as the week unfolds and embrace all the exciting things life brings your way.

3. Display your menu

This is part of the fun! Each weekend spend a little time to plan, create and dream up a new menu for the week. (Or, if you prefer to use my 12 week plans which are all prepared for you, join my online program at www.GetFitFeelFabulous.co.nz)

Write your menu out; for example on a whiteboard, chalk board, a laminated piece of paper, the glass of a framed picture or even onto a window. Previously I used a chalk board, but have since found that using whiteboard markers straight onto the glass of a picture frame, with a Monday to Sunday outline, is tidier and more visually appealing.

Do whatever works in your space. If you like the look you create with your menu, you will enjoy the process and keep it up!

I like to plan our week's meals straight onto my display menu which goes beside the fridge. Whatever you use, put it up somewhere prominent, in the kitchen or living area. Your whole family can get excited seeing the gorgeous menu that is coming up for the week. Just like a holiday, part of the enjoyment of eating is the anticipation! It also makes it easy to switch and change your menu by adding arrows to swap things or to strike a meal off if you unexpectedly get invited out.

4. Shop to your menu

Write your shopping list in conjunction with your weekly menu so a cohesive plan is set out while it is fresh in your mind. Have your menu in front of you and your pantry open so you can see exactly what is on hand and what you need to stock up on.

It is useful to tie your plan in with the seasonal produce and the weekly specials on offer. You can even start your meal plan ideas by looking up the specials online and basing your meals around what you find. It is wonderful what ideas come from selecting a key ingredient, for example you might see salmon, eggplants or whole chickens on sale and choose to base your meals around that for the coming week.

I tend to plan my menu with my laptop open on the kitchen counter while browsing online. This way I can easily check what's left in my pantry, fridge and freezer so it all ties in and saves time and money and sets me up for a delicious week ahead.

5. Simplify your shopping

I am a huge fan of ordering groceries online, and believe me I put off being converted for a long time, but now I wouldn't go back! It is incredibly convenient and again saves me so much time and money.

Online shopping is great value for a whole raft of reasons:

- You can price compare every single product with one glance (the price per 100g is the best tool for this).
- You avoid any extra unnecessary spending that often goes with wandering the aisles.
- You also avoid having children pester you for extras (if you usually shop with children.)
- You can see your total grocery bill as you go and can adjust it as desired before confirming payment, so you never get caught out going over budget at the checkout counter.
- Often products will be upgraded at no extra cost if the item you ordered was out of stock.

- With some supermarkets, when you purchase meat, seafood and the like by the kilo you almost always receive a larger portion than what you actually pay for (as they have to give you a fillet at least as large as you order).
- Sometimes you receive bonus vouchers and giveaway products.
- You save on fuel costs getting to and from the grocery store (if you get it delivered).
- Often there are specials offering free delivery or cash coupons to offset any delivery fees. Alternatively, you can order and simply collect the groceries when you're next driving by.

What I love most of all however is that it saves so much time. I hardly ever forget things, as I can refer to my pantry and the recipes for the week while ordering, and the website reminds me of staple items I normally get, which I may have missed. It is bliss having groceries delivered straight to my kitchen, all chilled and frozen as opposed to the travel time, shopping time, check out time, loading and unloading time it would take me. (Yes you could argue that this would add exercise into my day but I prefer a 15 minute focused workout than 90 minutes shopping!)

One downside I find is not personally selecting the produce. I do always add comments for my personal shopper, for example to select half ripe and half green bananas. However, nothing beats being able to browse your local market and select what looks fresh and smells amazing that day. One exception I recommend, if you have the time available, is to shop for your fresh produce at your local market.

6. Batch cook by default

This is the secret weapon of how this system works and perhaps the single most important factor to reduce fuss. Set yourself up with a library of meals in your freezer and maintain it by bulk cooking as often as possible.

It takes almost no extra time to make a double, triple or even quadruple batch of curry, casserole, pasta dish, sauce, soup, pie or quiche. Any meal that will freeze well and/or which can be saved for lunch over the next day or two, should be intentionally cooked in bulk. This is all about having a simplicity and flow mindset.

Each time you cook a meal make it either a quick and easy meal that is on the table in minutes, or take a little more time and set aside future meals while preparing dinner. Sometimes you can do both as certain meals or ingredients, such as **Beef Bolognaise** or **Super Seven Sauce,** are both fast to prepare and make great frozen meal options as well.

Rather than having "boring leftovers" the very next night, simply label and freeze your extra meals and then enjoy a "twice as nice" night sometime over the coming two to three months. This is when you defrost a meal from the freezer to enjoy without having to cook. You will never need to order take-out meals again as you'll have your own lovingly cooked, preservative free, take-out meals ready to simply take out of the freezer!

By doing this routinely every week you can effectively cut out three or four nights' cooking and keep up the variety in your meals each week. I like to keep at least four or five frozen meals in my "library" at all times. This means there is always variety to work with and I will never be caught short without an easy dinner.

This system also saves you a lot of money as you can buy food in bulk. For years I used to buy meat in bulk and separate single meal portions into freezer bags to defrost and cook individually. Now I save that extra job (and cut down on freezer bags) as I cook the meals on a grand scale and get to enjoy them again later on.

There are very few meals that this doesn't work for. The only exceptions tend to be fresh fish dishes, delicate seafood, or meals like grilled steak that don't freeze well. For these sorts of meals I cook just enough for that dinner. Sometimes I also save leftovers for lunch the next day.

7. Set extra portions away first

This step is vital to make the entire system work. When you have planned to save portions for lunch and/or to freeze, always set them aside *before* serving dinner. Don't forget this essential step, otherwise your loving family and friends may decide to compliment your cooking by overeating the meal and not leaving enough of a portion to be useful for a future meal.

It's all about planning and communication. I find the easiest way to avoid this challenge is to either cook the extra meals in separate dishes, or to set them aside before dinner is placed on the table. It really makes a difference.

It is worthwhile investing in duplicate oven dishes to be able to easily prepare and cook two identical portions. This way you can freeze a pie, for example, in its dish ready to reheat directly in the oven.

I highly recommend a good supply of reusable freezer containers you can transfer meals into. Empty yoghurt containers work well for casseroles, dahl, curries, soups, meatballs and other flexible meals. You can discard them after a few uses if they have multiple labels.

You may also want to invest in a set of purpose made rectangular family dinner sized containers for meals that need to stay flat. Keep a permanent marker in your top kitchen drawer for labelling or you can use white sticky labels on containers.

Freezer bags and zip lock bags are also great. The sturdy ones can be washed out and re-used several times. Remember to label everything you freeze with the date and aim to use all meals within three months. Organise your freezer so your completed meals, baked items and meal ingredients are on separate shelves, so everything is easy to reach. (I cover more on this, including practical tips, in the section on freezing and thawing on **pg 94**.)

8. Shortcut

Always aim to shortcut from one meal to the next to create flow. When I make homemade pizza on a Friday night, I quadruple cook the sauce, freeze two portions for future meals and save one in the fridge for Saturday's lunch. The frozen portions of pizza sauce can be used with pasta, as a spread, in a stew, as part of my **4C Creamy Coconut Chicken Casserole** or simply for my next pizza night.

When cooking a roast, I cook extra vegetables and set them aside to use in salads, quiches or frittatas the next day. Roast kumara (sweet potato) and pumpkin (squash) are also lovely included in baking or in breakfasts such as my **Golden Pumpkin Pancakes**. Alongside this, I also make stock or soup from the roast bones and use the leftover roast meat in salads or wraps over the next two days.

If I'm serving rice, couscous or quinoa with a meal, I can cook extra and set some aside to serve in salads over the following two days.

9. Fresh is always first

When it comes to fruit and vegetables, structure your weekly menu to use fresh produce in preference to other options. Vegetables are only expensive if they get left in the bottom of the fridge to go soft and are eventually thrown out. Follow the principle of always first using any fresh produce that will soon be past its best. Learn how to substitute things into and out of meals to suit what's on hand. It is also important to store your vegetables well, checking your crisper drawer is at a good temperature, and storing things in separate containers as appropriate so nothing is unnecessarily crushed or blemished.

I don't often follow a recipe for salads but instead tend to make new salad creations each time, by simply matching food types, and taking care to use the produce that needs to be used up first. I explain how best to do this with my sensational salad blueprint system in part V so you never throw out valuable vegetables again.

At the start of the week (in relation to when you get groceries) always opt for fresh vegetables, and then start supplementing or replacing this with canned or frozen vegetable options as the week progresses. This ensures that you get maximum nutrients from the fresh produce, rather than leaving them sitting. Frozen and canned vegetables can be life savers when you want an instant salad or hot vegetables that will be ready in minutes.
Just make sure you don't use them when something fresh could have been substituted in their place.

10. Never waste food

Choose to have a zero food waste mentality by using fresh produce first, as mentioned in the point above. Save leftovers, even unexpected ones, and become creative in how you can use these in another salad, sauce or meal. Even small amounts of leftover sauce can be frozen into ice cube trays and stored in labelled zip lock bags for future soups and sauces.

Ice cube trays are also great for storing flavour enhancers. Chop up excess fresh herbs, ginger or chilli, half-fill the trays, then top up with water, stock or wine and freeze them. Similarly when limes and lemons are in abundance you can zest and juice them, and freeze the zest and juice as ice cubes, or put the dry zest directly into a zip lock bag and use for an instant flavour hit while cooking.

Any vegetables or meats that might otherwise go off can be frozen or made into soups. If you have excess garden produce from your own or friends' gardens, look up ways to bottle, preserve or make them into sauces. Lots of green vegetables can be blanched (cooked briefly in boiling water then rinsed in cold water) and frozen in plastic bags. Root vegetables can be roasted or cooked and mashed into purees and frozen in muffin trays, then added to casserole, curries and soups, or simply reheated as accompaniments once defrosted.
See pg 234 for a complete freezer storage guide.

It's convenient to have homemade produce available all year knowing it has been frozen when it was in season and still full of nutritional goodness. You can even buy seasonal produce in bulk when it is inexpensive expressly in order to preserve or freeze it. All these tips do wonders for your food budget!

11. Enjoy a weekly cook-up

Weekend afternoons are a great time to put on your favourite music and multitask by cooking, baking and preparing meals for the week ahead. If you have children you can make it a fun, interactive time, building memories while teaching them how to nourish themselves.

I recommend baking snacks such as muffins, slices and biscuits in batches ready to freeze. Simply place them into zip lock bags or containers and place in the freezer. You can then remove them one at a time and they will thaw in time for your morning snack. It's nice to have a wide variety of baking on hand which is easy to achieve by making a different batch or two each weekend and eating a little of each type during the week. It is also handy having baking for unexpected guests or to give away to a friend or neighbour when needed.

Your cook-up doesn't need to be limited to only baking. It's a great time to make sauces and condiments, and to bulk cook meals or soups ahead of time so that your busy work week is stress free and streamlined. Clear out the fridge of anything that is nearly past its best and incorporate it into a meal. Almost anything can go into a salad, soup or stir fry and often you will invent amazing meals by using up what's on hand!

Step by Step Menu Planning

Using the principles just outlined, here is a step by step process to help you create perfect menus, tailored to fit your life, week after delicious week.

As you learn this system you will find it flows very quickly and you will be able to do it in your head in a matter of minutes. To start out, however, I recommend putting pen to paper and going through the process step by step until it becomes second nature.

Start with a blank page with a Monday to Sunday grid with three rows, and spaces to add the extra information as set out below.

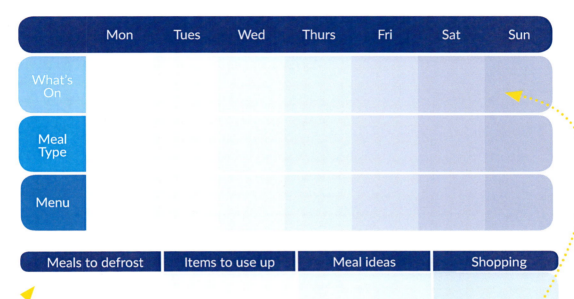

1. Start by adding any events, meetings or outings coming up this week in the "What's On" row.

2. Decide which nights you want to cook and which nights you want to have off and plan the type of meal that will suit your week. Add this to the "Meal Type" row.

    - On the nights when you have limited time, plan for either:
        - A defrosted meal
        - A quick and easy dinner (e.g. one you can cook in 5-10 minutes)
        - A meal that cooks itself (e.g. in a slow cooker, or a one pot wonder that takes very little prep time).
    - On the nights when you have more time you can plan for meals that may take a little more effort, and if possible, a recipe you can cook in bulk.

3. Next, check which meals you have in your freezer ready to defrost and what items you have in your fridge or pantry that need to be used up. Jot these down under "Meals to defrost" and "Items to use up".

real food less fuss 73

4. By now you may have meal ideas coming to mind. If not, refer to your favourite recipes (which are great to keep in a folder in the kitchen) and to any new recipes you want to try. Get ideas from cookbooks, magazines or the internet. Jot down the ideas you have for this week in the "Meal Ideas" column. To avoid confusion I recommend starting with no more than five or six ideas. Think of balancing out the main ingredients over the course of the week in relation to the frozen meals you have on hand.

5. Now you can add the meals for the week into the "Menu" row of your week's plan. Start with the meals you will defrost, then plan which meals you will batch cook. Lastly add any quick and easy meals or ones that cook themselves, writing each down under the appropriate day of the week column.

6. Make sure you have enough batch cooking sessions to restock your freezer and note down if you plan to do a double, triple or quadruple batch. (If you quadruple cook, you might only need to do one big batch and still be able to defrost several meals each week, all the while maintaining a well-stocked "library" in your freezer.)

7. Once your weekly menu is in place, create your shopping list to suit the meals you've planned. Think about what you might use in your salads to compliment the meals and of course stock up on your regular staples and plenty of fresh produce.

8. Now write your menu up and display it for the week so you and your family can enjoy looking forward to it!

In this example on the opposite page:

- You start the week with a variety of five meals ready in your freezer.
- On Monday you will be home late, so chose a quick and easy dinner using the beef bolognaise from the freezer along with lettuce wraps (which need to be used early in the week so they don't perish).
- Tuesday you use up the cauliflower and triple cook the curry.
- Wednesday you defrost the meatballs and cook extra rice which is set aside for a quick and easy egg fried rice dinner on Thursday, when you'll be home late.
- On Saturday you have dinner guests coming but are also out for the afternoon with sports, so you plan a slow cooked lamb tajine meal which also uses the figs that you noticed in the pantry.
- On Sunday you have extra time to again do a double or triple batch, so you plan to make fish pies using up the potatoes. This is a better option than the fish and chips idea as a fish pie is one of the few fish meals that freezes well.
- You also plan to do a batch of lemon slice on the Sunday and freeze the majority. If you run out of time to do this, then you could simply freeze the lemon juice and zest and delay this baking till the following week.
- If Sunday does turn out to be too busy to cook, it will be easy to defrost either the pasta sauce, chicken casserole or lasagne for dinner instead that night and skip doing the fish pies until the next night.
- If however you follow this plan as it stands, next week you'll still have the pasta sauce, chicken casserole and lasagne in the freezer along with the chicken curries and fish pies.

Here is an example of a completed menu using this system:

	Mon	Tues	Wed	Thurs	Fri	Sat	Sun
What's On	Home Late		Meeting at 7pm	Home Late	Out for Dinner	Friends for Dinner Afternoon Sport	
Meal Type	Quick and Easy or Defrost	Batch Cook	Defrost	Quick and Easy		Cooks Itself Meal	Batch Cook
Menu	Lettuce Wraps with Bolognaise (defrost)	Chicken Cauliflower Curry	Pork Meatballs with Rice	Egg Fried Rice		Lamb Tajine	Potato Top Fish Pie

Meals to defrost	Items to use up	Meal ideas	Shopping
Beef Bolognaise Pasta Sauce Pork Meatballs in Sauce Chicken Casserole Lasagne	Cauliflower Lettuce Potatoes Dried Figs Lemons	Curry – to use up cauliflower Salmon – as quick meal or with friends? Lamb Tajine – with friends? Fish Pie or Fish n Chips – to use up potatoes?	Chicken Thighs Rice, Eggs, Lamb, Fish Fillets, Fruit, Vegetables, Nuts/Seeds, Yoghurt etc

real food less fuss

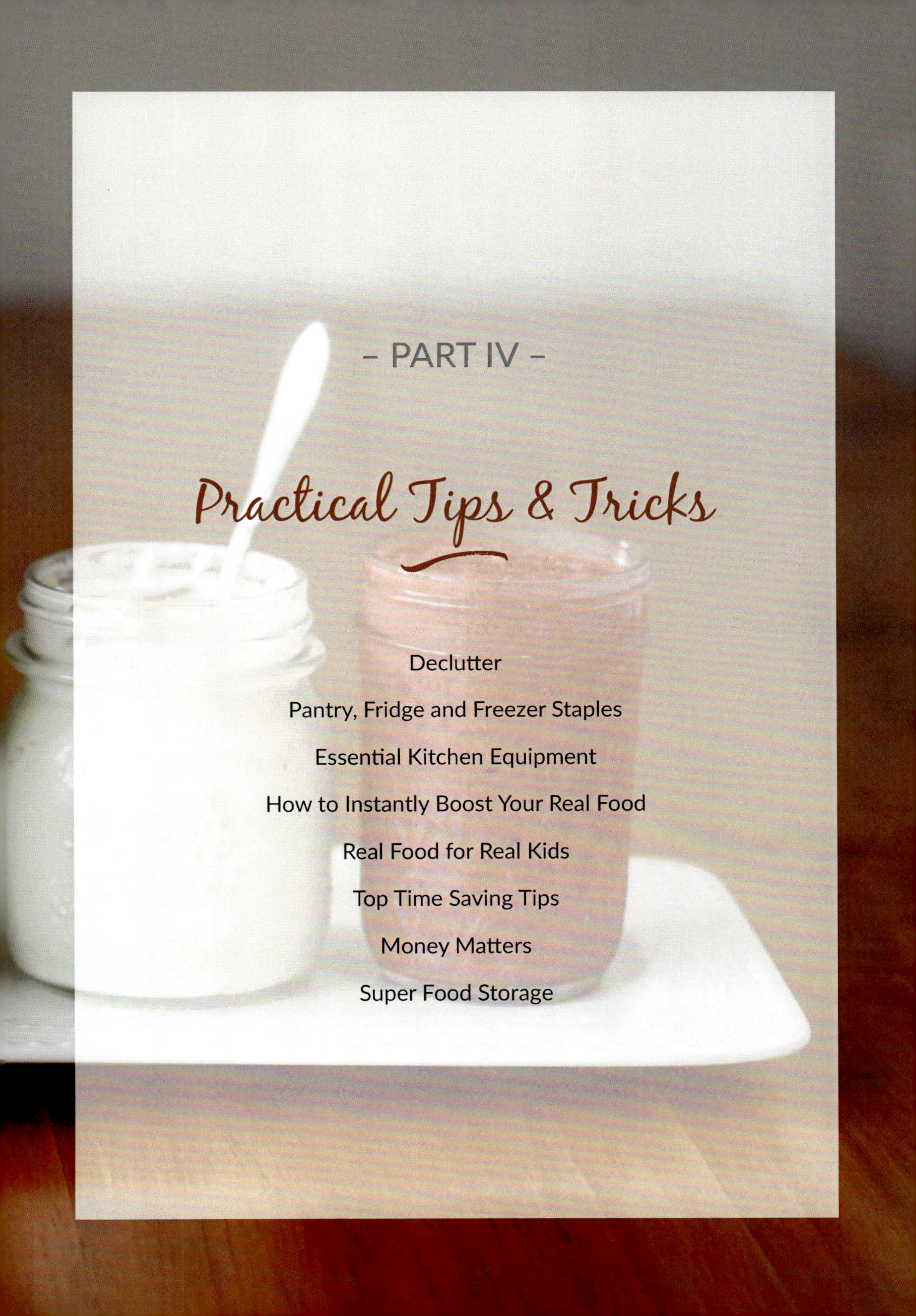

– PART IV –

Practical Tips & Tricks

Declutter

Pantry, Fridge and Freezer Staples

Essential Kitchen Equipment

How to Instantly Boost Your Real Food

Real Food for Real Kids

Top Time Saving Tips

Money Matters

Super Food Storage

Declutter

Establishing new habits starts with letting go of old ones.

A good way to start your real food journey is by becoming familiar with what you currently stock in your kitchen and making clear choices on what to keep and what to let go of. Plan a day and a time to do a complete pantry, fridge and freezer declutter.

To do this set aside two hours, emptying everything from your pantry onto your kitchen counter or a cleared dining table. This gives you a great chance to give your pantry a lovely spring clean. Do that first and let it dry out and air.

Sort through all of the packets, cans and products you have, reading through the labels and referring back to the information on food labels in Part I. Put back into your newly cleaned pantry all the plain and simple real food products (remember, those are the ones with just a few ingredients which closely resemble their original form.) Set aside anything that is less than desirable; e.g. those with long lists of ingredients, unrecognisable names, high amounts of added sugar, and any that contain trans fats or other unwanted additives. Either throw them straight out, or set them aside on a separate shelf, if disposing of them seems too drastic.

Over time you can work on replacing those items one by one with wholefood alternatives. You may feel more comfortable giving things away, or donating unopened items to your local food bank, if you prefer. Remember, once you are making your own delicious snacks, cereals, sauces and meals from wholesome ingredients, you won't ever need store bought ones again!

Pantry, Fridge and Freezer Staples

A well-stocked pantry, fridge and freezer makes eating well incredibly easy.

Here are some of the things I most recommend you have on hand. Don't feel that you have to rush out and buy the whole list at once. Over time you can add a few items each week with the confidence you will use them regularly now you are adopting a real food approach to life!

Pantry Staples

- Fruits – I find it best to keep a mixture of fruit in an easily accessible place to be used over two to three days with the remainder in the fridge. Some fruit such as bananas are best kept at room temperature, with spares kept in a dark cupboard so they ripen more slowly. When you want them to ripen put them together with your apples and other fruit. Splitting a large bunch this way helps some ripen faster than others and reduces wastage.

- Vegetables – onions, garlic, pumpkin (squash), potatoes, kumara (sweet potato). Store onions and garlic away from other vegetables and store all of them in a dark cool dry place.

- Canned/puréed vegetables – diced tomatoes, tomato paste, chickpeas (garbanzo beans), lentils, corn, beetroot (beets), kidney beans, cannellini beans or bean mixes.

- Canned fish – salmon, tuna in spring water, flavoured tuna.

- Free range eggs – keep what you will use that week at room temperature and the rest in the fridge.
- Wholemeal pasta – lasagne sheets, spaghetti, penne.
- Grains and grain substitutes – brown rice, quinoa, wholemeal couscous.
- Dry lentils – red, brown, puy.
- Cereals – whole oats, cut oats, bran, all bran.
- Flours/meals – wholemeal flour, buckwheat flour, spelt flour, almond meal, LSA (ground linseed, sunflower and almond).
- Baking needs – baking powder, baking soda, cornflour, cacao or cocoa powder, desiccated coconut, dried dates and sultanas.
- Raw natural nuts – almonds, cashews, walnuts, Brazil nuts.
- Seeds – sesame, sunflower, pumpkin (pepitas), chia.
- Sweeteners – honey, pure maple syrup, rice malt syrup.
- Herbal teas.
- Vinegars – apple cider, balsamic, red wine and white vinegar.
- Oils/fats – extra virgin olive oil, avocado oil, coconut oil, butter. Store butter in a butter dish at room temperature so it's easy to spread. Top it up from the fridge as needed.
- Sauces – soy sauce, Worcestershire sauce, fish or oyster sauce, canned coconut milk and cream.
- Ground spices – cumin, coriander, curry powder, sweet paprika, garam masala, turmeric, chilli powder, cinnamon and ground ginger.
- Dried herbs – basil, oregano, bay leaves, and Tuscan seasoning. Note, I recommend using fresh herbs from your herb garden or pots as much as possible. Nothing beats their flavour when they are freshly picked, but dried herbs are great to have on standby.
- Salt and pepper – always grind peppercorns and salt in a mill when at the dinner table. Not all salt is created equal so look for great tasting varieties such as Himalayan rock salt or French *fleur de sel* a high quality hand harvested sea salt.
- Above all, stock your pantry with love. It's all any household really needs!

Freezer

- Homemade liquid stock or broth.
- Homemade baked goods – a mixture of different muffins, slices and biscuits.
- Complete cooked meals in family or individual portions.
- Meal components such as sauces, ready to form the base of a meal.
- Blueberries and other mixed berries.
- Frozen vegetables – peas, corn, beans, vegetable mixes.
- Wholemeal grainy bread.
- Lemon and lime juice and zest.
- Grated or sliced ginger.
- Kaffir lime leaves, bay leaves.

See advice on how best to store, defrost and use freezer items on **pg 94**.

Fridge

- Lots and lots of fresh seasonal salad and cooking vegetables, such as: artichoke, asparagus, cabbage, carrots, cauliflower, celery, corn, cucumber, baby spinach leaves, beetroot (beets), bok choy, broccoli, Brussel sprouts, capsicum (bell pepper), chilli pepper, eggplant (aubergine), green beans, kale, leek, lettuce, mixed greens, mushrooms, radishes, silver beet (Swiss chard), snow peas, spinach, spring onion (scallion), sprouts, tomato, watercress, courgette (zucchini).
- Fresh seasonal fruit that is best kept chilled such as apples, pears, citrus and stone fruits.
- Fresh ginger root.
- Natural Greek yoghurt and labneh.
- Wholegrain and Dijon mustard.
- Vinaigrette in a jar.
- Milk – of your choice e.g. whole cow's milk, almond milk, coconut milk.
- Butter.
- Cheese block – tasty, edam.
- Other cheeses – parmesan block, ricotta, feta.
- Condiments – hummus, harissa, pesto, nut butter, date puree.

Essential Kitchen Equipment

The right equipment makes the task easy. Here are the kitchen items I most recommend you invest in and some nifty tips to ensure you get the most from them.

Knives
- Large chef's knife
- Paring knife
- Bread knife
- Knife sharpener
- Knife steel

Get the best chef's knife you can afford. A high quality one will last a lifetime and you will use this for almost all your chopping. A paring knife lets you deal with precision tasks such as peeling, trimming and slicing fruit. A bread knife has a serrated blade and is not only useful for bread but makes short work of tomato and citrus as well.

It's worth visiting a speciality knife shop and seeking advice on how to keep your knives sharp.

I absolutely recommend keeping your knives on a wall-mounted magnetic knife strip. This provides ease of use and will keep your knives sharp and your fingers safe. Never store sharp knives in a drawer unless they have a blade cover. They are a hazard and will blunt easily. Also, never clean them in the dishwasher, it will also blunt the blade.

Chopping boards	Two or more large wooden boards. Designate one for raw meat preparation and one for vegetables. You may even want separate boards for poultry and seafood, but these aren't essential if you take care to wash your boards well between uses.
Pots and pans - A large fry pan - 3-4 pots of various sizes and a steamer - A large stock pot	It's worth investing in a good quality fry pan. Their weight is often a good indicator of their worth. Thick based ones will hold their heat far better, giving more even cooking. You will use your cookware so much over the years that it's important to stick with a quality brand that will last. I really like Stoneline cookware which is very hard wearing, highly non-stick and easy to clean. We've used their set of pots and pans for several years now and in spite of some excellent attempts, have never burnt a meal. You also want an extra large, thick-bottomed stock pot for making stocks, soups and for bulk cooking. Avoid any cheap non-stick varieties which can be unsafe.
Food processor	A sturdy large capacity food processor with an S blade is incredibly useful for making a range of condiments, desserts and wholefood snacks. It will most likely be the most expensive food preparation tool you own and it is worth getting a good one that will last. They generally come with various blade attachments which allow you to slice, dice or grate large quantities of vegetables – great for salads and when making sauces.
Kitchen scales	These are important for accuracy when making bread.

Various utensils

- Large spoon
- Slotted spoon
- Ladle
- Fish Slice
- Whisk
- Tongs
- Spatula
- Potato masher
- Can opener
- Pastry brush
- Peeler

I recommend getting a rail and hooks for these to save space and for ease of use. You can get a nice matching set and create a feature on your kitchen wall that will look great alongside your knife strip!

Flavour essentials

- Large box grater
- Hand held parmesan grater
- Hand held zester
- Lemon/lime juicer
- Garlic roller
- Garlic crusher
- Pepper mill
- Rock salt mill

Get a really sturdy box grater with a comfortable handle.

A light parmesan grater is good for use at the table.

A hand held flip top juicer is a superb pip free way to get all the juice out of citrus fruits.

A garlic roller is a simple silicone tube the size of a very fat cigar. It allows you to roll garlic out of its skin in seconds when you want diced garlic. Alternatively you can crush cloves directly in your garlic crusher with the skin on (it really works!)

Straining

- Colander
- Fine sieve
- Muslin cloth

Colanders are great for draining vegetables and pasta.

A really fine sieve is important for things like rinsing quinoa prior to cooking and for straining stock. Muslin is handy when making labneh or sprouts.

Baking ware - 2 Loaf tins - 2 round cake tins - 2 muffin trays	Good quality non-stick tins and trays. I prefer spring form cake tins which make it a dream to get cakes and cheesecakes out.
Wire cooling rack	Useful for cooling baking and homemade bread.
2 Roasting dishes	Great to spread vegetables out to crisp them up.
2-4 Baking trays	For bulk baking and pizza making.
Large casserole dish with a lid	It is great to have one which can go from stove top to oven, e.g. with oven proof handles, which allows you to brown meat and retain all of the flavour without having to change pans or create more washing up.
Baking dishes - 1-2 Large oblong dishes - 2 Square dishes	I like to get matching sets of these for double batch cooking. You can purchase ones with plastic storage lids for ease of freezing complete meals. They can later be reheated directly in the dish, (minus the lid of course!)
Storage containers	A variety of glass, stainless or BPA-free plastic storage containers and zip lock bags.
Serving dishes/bowls and platters	Whatever style takes your fancy. When it looks great it increases everyone's anticipation of, and respect for, the meal you've prepared.

A note on dinnerware	Serving sizes have increased along with the size of our plates. Opt for smaller serving plates that help avoid overeating. It is more visually satisfying eating from a smaller plate which appears full than from a larger plate that appears half empty.
Measuring cups	To be honest, I tend to just use the cup and ½ cup measures and guesstimate the rest.
Nest of mixing bowls	Always handy to have. Include at least one large mixing bowl and a smaller bowl suitable for warming e.g. Pyrex.

Optional Extras:

Salad spinner	A kitchen essential all over France – and becoming so throughout the world. A salad spinner ensures your washed salad greens are dry so that your delicious vinaigrette is able to properly coat the ingredients in your salad. Alternatively, you can spin them in a clean tea towel outside.
Stick blender	This can be really handy for making smooth sauces and soups. You can make do with a food processor but a stick blender saves loads of time and washing up.
Spice grinder	Wonderful for making your own ground spices and spice mixes, should you be so inclined. It is incredibly satisfying and will make your home smell amazing but certainly isn't essential when you first start out.
Rice cooker	An easy way to have perfect rice every time and to keep it hot before serving. You can however cook rice in a pot by the absorption method. Just remember to avoid removing the lid or stirring the rice. The holes that appear act like steam vents and allow the rice to cook evenly.
Slow cooker	Perfect if you are out all day and get home just before dinner time. Five minutes' preparation in the morning allows you to return home to a ready cooked meal.
Small ramekins	These can be nice to have for serving fancy individual desserts and are an attractive way to serve extra flavour enhancers like fresh herbs at the table. They are also great for managing portion sizes of desserts.

How to Instantly Boost Your Real Food

This synopsis ties together much of what has been discussed in the book so far. It provides lots of tricks which will immediately increase your real food intake. Pick and choose from these simple strategies and substitutions to eat more natural, nutrient dense food!

Boost Your Vegetables

- Have a salad entrée before every meal, as well as serving vegetables alongside or as part of your main course.
- Base a meal around a vegetable. For example do stuffed butternut, try homemade oven baked beetroot (beets), carrot and parsnip chips, cook mushrooms with a balsamic reduction or make ratatouille. Try out new recipes that make one or more vegetables the main event.
- Smuggle vegetables into meals whenever possible. Grate, blend, thinly slice, layer. This is not just something to try for your kids; it is a wonderful way to get more vegetables into the whole family's diet and to expose your palate to more delicious nutritious food.
- Aim for two different coloured vegetables at lunch and three different coloured vegetables at dinner time. This is a simple visual reminder to help you get at least five servings in each day.
- Snack on raw vegetable sticks. For example celery, carrots, capsicum (bell pepper), cucumber or even small broccoli and cauliflower florets, are delicious, along with tasty condiments such as hummus or pesto.

Snacks and Sweets

- Make simple substitutions to adapt your favourite recipes. For example swap white bleached flour for wholemeal flour. Swap refined sugar for **Date Puree**, maple syrup, honey or fresh or stewed fruit.
- Always keep a mixture of 2-4 different types of nutritious home baking in the freezer for lunch boxes, snacks, unexpected guests or to take to a social occasion.
- For dessert, enjoy homemade **Unbelievably Good Ice Cream** (made from bananas) with dark chocolate grated on top, or homemade **Labneh** with cinnamon, fruit and sliced almonds.
- Snack on whole fruits, vegetables, nuts/seeds or your wholesome homemade baking rather than buying biscuits, cakes or slices.

Better Breakfasts

- Mix up **Quick Natural Muesli** and **Bircher Muesli** in bulk to last for a week or two. Store it with a half cup measure to manage your serving sizes.
- Use natural Greek yoghurt rather than the flavoured, sugar laden varieties.
- Learn how to cook eggs to perfection. They are great as a quick and simple complete meal. Poaching eggs is my favourite way to enjoy them and is easy to do once you know the secret to keeping them together, which I share on **pg 138**.

- Make your own delicious **Wholesome Homemade Bread** and store it pre-sliced in the freezer.
- Break away from the traditional view of breakfast and remember that you can eat anything at any time of the day should you so desire. Enjoy your greens and vegetables at breakfast time such as in a green smoothie, roasted vegetables, fried halved tomatoes or fresh avocados.

Prepare for Success

- Set up your salad bar at the start of the week by washing and spinning dry your lettuce and preparing your vegetables in handy containers. Mix up a jar of vinaigrette to last throughout the week so salads are the easy go-to option that can be thrown together in seconds.
- Learn and use a variety of different ways to cut, slice, dice and peel your vegetables to add interest to your meals and salads.
- Triple or quadruple batch cook every meal that you can and keep your library of meals well stocked so you never get caught out needing to order takeaways.
- Make up meal components such as pasta sauces, bolognaise, chilli, casseroles and vegetables and freeze them in easy to use portions.
- Most of all, clear out any processed foods you don't need and ensure your pantry, fridge and freezer are stocked with delicious whole foods so they are on hand for ready use.

Maximise Flavour

- Use cooking methods that concentrate rather than dissipate flavours such as roasting, slow cooking, browning meat and reducing sauces down to enrich their flavour.
- Have easy flavour enhancers on hand to boost the taste of every meal. For example:
  - Dry toast a batch of raw nuts and/or seeds and store them in an airtight container for the week to add to salads.
  - Keep lemon/lime zest and juice, and sliced ginger in the freezer.
  - Grow fresh herbs and use them at every meal.
  - Keep a few tasty condiments/sauces and a block of parmesan cheese in the fridge to add a little something to your dinner.
  - Always have freshly ground pepper and good quality salt on hand.

Real Food for Real Kids

As a parent I understand the challenges of getting small people on board with nutritious food choices. Here are some practical ideas to positively influence your children to enjoy more real food.

- Grow your own herbs and vegetables and get your children involved in the process.
- Give each child a small section of the garden which belongs to them. They will be proud to serve up and eat "their" peas, carrots or corn at the dinner table.
- If an entire garden seems too much, then start out with some herbs in pots and plant a lemon tree.
- Involve your children in food preparation. From age two they can help with picking produce, putting it into a bowl or basket and washing it. From age five onwards they can start to learn knife skills with supervision and guidance. Mushrooms are a good option to start working with before progressing to firmer produce.
- Take your children shopping at farmers' markets and teach them to look for the freshest produce. Make an experience out of smelling the different herbs and spices.
- Have a salad entrée together as a family. This exposes your children to a mixture of different vegetables. You can include some child-friendly options such as cheese cubes, diced apples and cherry tomatoes to make the whole thing more appealing.
- Make meal times relaxed and fun rather than a battle by having a consistent approach which could include a motto such as "In our family we taste everything."
- Keep offering foods multiple times in different ways. A child may not like grated carrot but may love carrot sticks for example (or vice versa).
- It can take 18 tastes before a new food is appreciated, so persevere and try things out in different ways: e.g. kumara (sweet potato) chips, roasted broccoli, eggplant (aubergine) pizza, celery smiles.
- Remind your children that they may just not like this food "yet" but that their taste buds are changing and learning all the time.
- Making animal or face shapes on the plate or giving food fun names can help young children get on board to try things out.
- Blend extra vegetables into sauces and combine these into your meals to boost the nutritional value.
- Be mindful of your language and the way that you speak about food. Teach your children that certain foods are super nutritious and will help them become strong and healthy and this is why we eat mostly these foods.
- Avoid labelling foods as "good" or "bad", simply reinforce that we always make sure we eat enough nutritious food to fuel our body well.
- Make a point of ensuring everyone thanks the cook before getting down from the table.
- Get an ice block mould and make homemade ice blocks with leftover smoothie, chai tea, banana ice cream or even just pieces of fruit topped up with fruit juice.

- Make birthday parties healthier by icing birthday cakes with my **Secret Chocolate Mousse** recipe. Serve fruit kebabs, popcorn and natural wholefood baking and fill take-home bags with stickers, stamps and pens rather than lollies.

- When you do need a special dessert, opt for naturally sweetened fruit based options such as **Perfect Pumpkin Pie**, **Lemon Lime Pistachio Cheesecakes** or **Banoffee Pie**.

Lunchbox Tips

- It is important to include a good source of protein in every lunch. (This is often lacking with a lot of lunches being predominantly carbohydrate based, which can lead to blood sugar spikes and lows, creating tiredness and brain fog.) Young minds and bodies need the building blocks from protein to function well. This could be a boiled egg, raw nuts, **Quinoa Quiche**, chicken drumsticks, meatballs or leftover meat from the previous night's dinner.

- Include both fresh fruit and child friendly vegetables such as snow peas, corn, cherry tomatoes or carrot, cucumber or capsicum (bell pepper) sticks along with a dipping sauce such as **Harissa**, **Labneh** or **Parsley and Basil Pesto**. Celery sticks topped with **Nut Butter** are popular as well.

- Think outside the square for the sandwich component of their lunch. Use wholemeal pita pockets, wraps, homemade bread, scones, seedy crackers or pizza.

- Don't be afraid to replace the traditional sandwich altogether with leftovers from dinner. For example roast meat and vegetables, kebabs and salad, pasta bake, **Apple and Pork Rolls**, or **Risotto That Cooks Itself**.

- As a treat include a piece of homemade baking such as a muffin, biscuit, slice or even a **Golden Pumpkin Pancake**.

- In winter a sealable thermos cup with a soup is a lovely option along with some **Wholesome Homemade Bread**.

- The easiest way to avoid lots of packets in your child's lunchbox is to keep a variety of homemade lunch items in your freezer so you always have healthy protein options and baking ready to go, as well as condiments in the fridge. Along with some fresh fruit and vegetables lunch will be quick and easy to put together.

Top Time Saving Tips

Wouldn't we all love to have more time? These tips can save you hours each week, giving you the freedom of more quality time to do the things you love.

Planning and Shopping

- Open the pantry, look over the fridge and plan your meals for the week ahead, and write them directly onto your menu to go up on the wall.
- Do your online shopping at the same time while everything is at the top of your mind, checking the pantry so you don't forget any necessary items.
- If you find yourself stuck for inspiration, make meal planning into a game by writing your favourite meals out on cards or ice cream sticks (which you can buy in variety stores) and draw them out of a jar one at a time to add to your meal plan. Your kids are likely to enjoy taking charge of this for you. You could colour code your meals vegetarian, fish, chicken and meat, or just leave them all identical so it's a total lucky dip!

Cooking and Preparation

- Start with as much clear space as you can.
- Always start with a sharp knife.
- Use the chef's technique of *mise en place*, (putting in place) which involves prepping your meal components prior to the busy service time.
- Do one step at a time and work systematically (e.g. halve and quarter all the apples, then de-core them all, then slice them all.) This is how chefs are taught to work as efficiently as possible.
- When you prepare vegetables for your main meal, prepare your salad vegetables at the same time. You can even dice, slice and grate vegetables in advance for your salads over the next few days and store them fresh in separate containers or plastic bags in the fridge.
- Use your food processor to chop vegetables when you are doing a large amount. Get familiar with the different blades or attachments for grating, slicing and so on.
- If you need hot water, fill and boil the jug before you start cooking and use the boiling water rather than heating cold water in a pot on the stovetop.
- Heat your pans/oven before you start cooking.
- Roast large chunks of pumpkin (squash) with the skin on and scoop out the flesh rather than spending time chopping the skins off. For most varieties, the skin can also be eaten as it softens once cooked.
- When doing a canned salad keep the cans in the fridge so they are pre-chilled and the salad can be served instantly.
- Put whole cloves into your garlic crusher, skin and all, and crush away. The flesh and juice all comes out and it saves time, hassle and garlic flavoured fingers.
- If you do want sliced, diced or whole garlic, use a garlic roller (silicon tube) to instantly remove the skin.

- When roasting or steaming, cook extra amounts to store in the fridge for another meal the next day or to label and freeze as a ready meal ingredient for another night.
- The biggest time saver is of course triple and quadruple batch cooking meals, and meal components to give yourself entire nights off cooking. Make it your default to do this whenever possible.

Storage Systems

- Keep a permanent marker pen in your kitchen drawer and label and date everything as you freeze it.
- Invest in good quality sets of containers and zip lock bags suitable for freezing individual and family size meals and meal components. Get smaller bags or containers suitable for snacks and lunches. Keep them tidy and organised in your cupboard for ease of use.
- Store similar things together in your freezer to make them easy to find. Designate specific areas for complete meals, meal ingredients and flavour enhancers, frozen berries and vegetables, bread, stock and raw meat. Make sure everyone knows how your freezer storage system works and remember to rotate things to the bottom or the back as you store them, so older items are easier to find when defrosting.
- Ideally I recommend investing in an upright freezer with shelves or drawers which make things much more accessible and mean you can easily rotate frozen items. You may be able to make do with the freezer that is part of your refrigerator. However once you get into the habit of freezing extra cooked meals the storage capacity may be too restrictive. If you use a chest freezer, use large plastic storage cubes to separate things out.

Money Matters

We all want to make our budget go as far as possible. Here are my top tips to enjoy great food at a great price.

Savvy Switches

- Make your own takeaways. Homemade curries, gourmet fish and chips, pizza, sausage rolls and the like can all be delicious, healthy and very cost effective alternatives to the take out variety.
- Make your own staples such as bread, cereal and condiments using the basic whole ingredients which are much cheaper by weight. When you get into the routine of doing this in bulk regularly it doesn't take a lot of time.
- Every time you have a roast, set a pot of stock or bone broth to simmer using the bones and scraps. It makes delicious homemade stock.
- Halve the meat, double the vegetables. For plenty of meals you can increase the nutrition and save dollars by reducing the proportion of meat and adding in extra canned, frozen or seasonal fresh vegetables.
- Replace meat altogether with legumes such as chickpeas (garbanzo beans), lentils and beans which are filling and incredibly nutritious. If you are concerned about objections from family members try weaning them onto this by starting out half and half with legumes and meat. Adapt it gradually over time.

Shopping Savers

- When purchasing meat, buy it in bulk while it is on special and cook it in large batches, freezing meal components or complete meals.
- Buy meat and poultry close to its best before date when it is at a further reduced price. Cook it within the dates outlined and freeze leftovers.
- Opt for some of the less expensive cuts of meat. These are great for slow cooking to create tender delicious meals, which are also freezer friendly.
- Shop online so you can quickly and easily compare the price by weight, make the most of specials and avoid unnecessary purchases.
- Avoid pre-packaged small servings of things such as raisins or crackers. Simply buy the larger packet, keep it in an airtight container and put appropriate servings into re-usable zip lock bags or small containers as needed. This cuts down on a lot of unnecessary packaging, which is great for the planet as well as your budget.

Preparation

- Prepare lunches ahead of time and take them with you. Even if you eat at home, preparing your lunch in advance makes portion-control easy, plus it saves you time.
- Set up a lunch club with three colleagues where you each have a set weekday to provide lunch for four. Then you get to relax on the other days when they cater in turn for you.
- Rather than going out for a café lunch, pack a picnic. You may still choose to enjoy a hot drink or some other small dine-out item as a treat, but you avoid catering your whole meal at restaurant prices. The added benefit is controlling your food choices to make them more nutritious than what might have been on offer dining out.

Portion Sizes

- When going out for dinner with friends, invite them over for nibbles beforehand, or if it is just you and your partner going out share some nibbles and a drink together at home. This way you can take the edge off your appetite while controlling what you serve (for example vegetable sticks, hummus, olives, avocado on wholegrain crackers.) You also avoid paying restaurant prices for table breads, starters or drinks.
- Control your portion sizes. It may seem obvious, but it is worth pointing out that eating less saves you money. You may find it helpful to weigh or measure your food for a couple of weeks when you start to focus on adjusting your portions. Often we are unaware of the actual portion sizes we consume.
- Put vegetables on your plate first. This one simple habit tends to increase vegetable intake.
- If people tend to go for seconds out of habit, serve individual meals onto each person's plate rather than putting the serving dishes out on the table.
- Always set you planned leftovers aside before serving your meal. This is vital to ensure your double batch really does cover two entire meals.
- Serve slightly less than you think you want to eat. Enjoy that amount, then pause for a bit and reflect on whether you really need more. This way, even if you do decide to go back for seconds, you are less likely to overeat.

- Use smaller plates and bowls.
- Aim to eat until you are not quite full. You will quickly realise that your body really does feel much better when you avoid overeating.
- Take control of serving up your own portions and become familiar with the actual sizes you put on or into your plate, bowl or cup. Use the visual reminder of your own fist and palm. Your closed fist is the size of your stomach when empty.
- Fill up on vegetables. Many people grew up with the common saying "fill up on bread". Choose to replace this with "fill up on salad" and make it your new family motto.
- I have to mention salad entrées again as a first course of seasonal vegetables is great for your wallet as well as your waist! Once you have dressed your salad it is best consumed immediately, so it really encourages you to ensure it is all eaten before moving on to the main meal.
- Serve cereal using a ½ cup measure rather than pouring it from the packet, so you don't accidentally start serving yourself ever increasing portions.
- Use sandwich rather than toast bread, or with your own bread cut thinner slices.
- When it comes to treats, if you are presented with two or more treats – for example a dessert buffet or a latte and a piece of cake – choose to have one or the other rather than both. Consider how you want to feel afterwards and bear in mind that overindulging will give you a sugar rush and leave you feeling flat and lethargic afterwards.
- Most of all, whenever you do have a treat, eat it slowly and mindfully and savour every bite.

Waste Not Want Not

- Avoid food wastage by having a zero waste mentality. Planning your weekly meals ahead will ensure you rarely waste anything. You can also be flexible with recipes so as to add in any fresh produce that will soon be past its best. You can add extra vegetables to your main or make them part of your salad. If you have excessive amounts of something left over you may be able to preserve, bottle or freeze it on its own.
- Ginger shrivels up and goes mouldy if left in the fridge, so with fresh ginger, take any amount you won't use within a few days, peel it with a spoon, then grate or finely slice it into ice cube trays, top with water and freeze it.
- Zest and juice any lemons and limes you will not use within the next week. Spread the zest evenly among ice cube trays and fill with juice, or leave some sections with juice on its own.
- Chop fresh herbs and place in ice cube trays and cover with water, stock or wine. For each of these three examples, pop the cubes out once frozen and store them in labelled zip lock bags.
- If you do have unexpected leftovers, make them stretch to another meal, which saves you a whole night's dinner cost. Or if only a small serving remains, freeze it as an individual portion. Be mindful that the last two serving spoonfuls from the pot may not look like a lot, but it will likely be enough for lunch the next day or an easy frozen dinner for one person.

Super Food Storage

These tips explain the best ways to store, freeze and reheat food safely and for maximum enjoyment.

Storage

- Cover all food with a plate or in a sealed container before placing in the fridge.
- Never leave tinned food open in the fridge. Transfer any remaining amounts into a bowl or container to store.
- Store raw meat, fish and poultry at the bottom of the fridge. Ensure blood and juices do not drip onto other food.
- Cool hot food quickly. Cool food on the bench until the steam stops rising, then place it directly into the fridge on top of a plate, and later on into the freezer.
- Avoid placing too many hot items into the fridge at once as they may heat nearby items.
- Avoid leaving food any longer than 30 minutes at room temperature before chilling.
- Consume all leftovers placed in the fridge within two days.

Freezing

- Seal containers with as little air as possible; except for soups, stocks and casserole style meals with a high liquid content which will expand when frozen. In this case, leave a space at the top to allow for expansion.
- Where a meal has several separate components, it is best to freeze each component separately. Put pureed vegetables, green vegetables and the meat component into their own separate containers. This assists with reheating them in the best way and for the right timeframe for each component.
- It is best to cut your meal into portions or simply into halves or quarters before freezing. Examples would be with lasagne, quiche and frittatas, so either a small portion or the entire thing can be defrosted at a later date.
- For some meals such as pies or sausage rolls it can be beneficial to slightly undercook the portions you intend freezing so they can be reheated and crisped up in the oven at a later date without burning.
- Store different types of foods on different shelves or in separate areas of your freezer. Always store raw frozen foods at the bottom of the freezer and cooked meals and prepared meal ingredients at the top.
- If you have limited freezer space use plastic bags for things like muffins, cakes and biscuits and get sets of matching freezer containers of an appropriate size for family meals so they can be easily stacked.

- Label everything you put into the freezer and include the date you froze it.
- Consume complete meals within three months of freezing.
- You might like to keep a laminated list on the lid or side of your freezer. This way you can record down each meal as it is frozen and wipe it off as it is used. This serves as a quick "freezer-library" reference tool.

Thawing and Reheating

- Frozen raw foods that have been cooked can be refrozen. For example if you buy fresh chicken, then freeze it, you can thaw it out and cook it into a casserole and then freeze the casserole once. You can then thaw and reheat it to eat, but do not freeze and thaw it thereafter. Once the casserole is defrosted it needs to be eaten immediately or kept in the fridge and eaten within 2 days.
- Once food is thawed it must be cooked before re-freezing. For example if you thaw out some beef to do a meal but change your mind, it needs to go into the fridge to be cooked and eaten within two days. It cannot be re-frozen while it is raw.
- Homemade baking can thaw out at room temperature within a couple of hours. Individual muffins, slices or biscuits can go directly into lunch boxes frozen and they will be ready to eat by mid-morning.
- Thaw frozen meals in the fridge overnight for the following day. If thawing something on the counter ensure that it is placed in the fridge once almost thawed.
- Allow food to thaw completely before reheating.
- To speed up thawing, place the frozen package inside a sealed bag in the sink and cover with warm water. Change the water every 30 minutes until the food is thawed.
- Choose the best method of reheating (e.g. in a frypan, oven or microwave) depending on the type of meal and the quantity. Thick casserole dishes can take a long time to warm up in the oven; be sure to allow time for the meal to heat right through to the center. Individual portions can be reheated in the microwave if you are short on time.
- Always reheat food to steaming hot then allow it to cool slightly before eating. Food should reach 75° C or 165 °F to kill any bacteria.
- When reheating in the microwave, make sure you stir food periodically while heating so that the food is steaming throughout and not just on the edges.
- Garnish reheated meals with something fresh to keep them looking and tasting delicious, e.g. fresh herbs, diced chilli, ground pepper or grated parmesan.

General Food Safety

- Ensure that hands are regularly washed in hot soapy water during food preparation and dried on a hand towel or paper towel.
- Thoroughly clean all benches, cutting boards, and knives with hot soapy water.
- Use separate chopping boards, utensils and serving platters for ready-to-eat food, such as salad vegetables, and raw foods such as meat. This prevents cross contamination from raw foods to ready-to-eat foods. You may want to invest in different chopping boards for different foods.

– PART V –

Fresh and Delicious

Herbs and Spices

Creative Condiments

Sensational Salads

Great Vinaigrettes

Sensational Salad Blueprints

Make a Meal of It

Herbs and Spices

One of the keys to eating well and really enjoying nutritious food is to maximise the flavour of every meal so that it truly satisfies. Delicious meals are not complete without great herbs and spices. However, for some people it can be daunting to know which ones to use when and in what quantities.

Often people will add flavour to their cooking solely by adding a lot of fat, sugar and salt. Herbs and spices reduce the need for this as they boost flavour without any extra calories. Many also have health giving and healing properties. So increasing your knowledge and use of herbs and spices boosts both your enjoyment of food and your health.

One of the problems with a bland meal is that you can end up eating more in an attempt to feel satisfied. Conversely, a meal which is well seasoned with interesting flavours will be much more satisfying overall.

Having a good supply of the basic spices in your kitchen and knowing how to use them also saves you money. I recall as a young married couple that we regularly bought packet mixes which were essentially just a mixture of spices, salt and sugar. At the time we didn't realise there was no need for these as we could easily have made a similar mix ourselves without any extra additives.

Combining Flavours

Many people lack confidence or knowledge of which spices work well together and which best complement key meal ingredients. Understandably they worry that they might spoil an entire dish by adding something that doesn't tie in with the flavours.

About 10 years ago my husband Morrie, who loves to experiment, came up with a method of identifying which spice or ingredient will likely work with a meal before adding it. Tongue in cheek he has dubbed it the "taste and sniff" method. Essentially, this allows you to experiment with and learn to use herbs and spices with much less risk of ruining dinner. Taste and sniff works because our senses of smell (olfactory) and taste (gustatory) are fundamentally linked. This method provides a way of "tasting" what a spice or ingredient will do to your meal before you have actually added it, giving you a sense of whether you are about to spoil or improve your meal.

Here is how it works. When you are unsure whether two things will go together, simply taste a spoonful of what you have prepared thus far without swallowing it. While you hold it in your mouth allowing your taste buds to work, inhale the aroma of the next herb or spice. If the taste and smell work well together (and don't set off alarm bells for you) then go ahead and add it.

You can use taste and sniff to experiment to your heart's content. It is the best way to learn about flavours and will help you start working with a wider range of herbs and spices. Just remember not to sniff pepper or chilli powder!

Bear in mind that some spices pack a punch, so start by adding a little, and continue to taste and adjust as you go. One of the most important keys to great cooking is to taste your meal regularly as you cook. Even when you follow a recipe it is important to regard it as a guide, not a set of rules. The size of an ingredient or the strength of flavour of a spice may differ from the original, so be flexible and adapt everything to your own taste.

It is also important to season with salt at each stage of the cooking process. This creates a good depth of flavour, whereas adding salt only towards the end of cooking can mean you end up with salty tasting food. For example, salt the water you are boiling vegetables in, then salt them again before roasting. Pasta should be cooked in water that tastes like the sea. Meat and fish should be seasoned before cooking. Using adequate salt enhances flavour and means you will use less salt overall as you won't need to add extra at the table.

Sourcing Spices

The best place to get your spices are the stores where your local Asian or Indian community buy their bulk spices. You will find you can buy decent sized bags of a wide range of spices for a similar price to what you pay for just a little packet in the supermarket. A store with a high turnover will ensure you get fresh spices that retain their flavour. Get to know the owners, and ask for their recommendations. They will generally be more than happy to advise you.

My favourite ground spices to have on hand are: cumin, coriander, curry powder, sweet paprika, garam masala, turmeric, chilli powder, cinnamon and ground ginger.

If you don't already have these, get yourself this set as a starting point and experiment by including a recipe that uses one each week. As you become more familiar with spices and spice combinations you can branch out further and include things such as Chinese five spice, nutmeg, saffron, smoky paprika, chilli flakes, cloves, allspice and star anise.

The next step is to buy whole spices such as cardamom pods, cinnamon sticks and fennel, cumin and coriander seeds. Dry fry the seeds and grind your own spice mixes together in a spice or coffee grinder, or a mortar and pestle. Your home will smell amazing when you do this and it is incredibly satisfying making an authentic tasting curry, dahl or tajine from scratch. While this can add a bit more fuss, because of the time and effort required, making spice blends from scratch on a leisurely weekend and enjoying a delicious meal, is great food for the soul. So if it appeals to you, give it a go as time allows.

Fantastic Fresh Herbs

When it comes to herbs, I find that fresh is best and highly recommend growing your own. However, having some dried herbs in the pantry as a backup; such as basil, parsley, oregano, Tuscan seasoning and bay leaves, can be useful. They are particularly good for slowly cooked casseroles and soups. That being said, there is no substitute for fresh herbs, especially when it comes to garnishes and salads.

Nothing is fresher than when picked straight from the garden, full of minerals and vitamins to nourish you!

Even if you don't have a vegetable garden, herbs can easily be grown in pots or planter boxes outdoors or on your kitchen window. Just take care that they don't dry out if in raised containers, particularly if they get a lot of sun. If you protect them from wind and ensure they get enough water they should produce well for you.

The top herbs I would start out with are: parsley, mint, coriander (cilantro), chives and basil.

These flavoursome five are relatively easy to grow and will give you a quick payback as they are so versatile. The basil and coriander just need to be well protected from the wind. Also bear in mind, mint plants shoot out runners and spread easily. So plant your mint in a pot either above ground or dug down into the garden to help contain its roots. Make sure you have enough herb plants to keep up with your everyday use. To expand your repertoire of herbs look at additional options such as sage, thyme, rosemary and oregano.

As well as herbs, why not grow a few seasonal vegetables. Easy and fun ones to start out with include lettuce, spinach, cherry tomatoes and courgettes (zucchini). You can leave your lettuce and spinach plants in the ground and just pick as many leaves as you need for each salad or meal, to maximise freshness. I love the way cherry tomatoes and courgettes keep producing during a long period, so you can keep using the ongoing supply on a nightly basis. Remember to give the courgettes some space as they like to spread out and ramble.

Tending a garden is a great project to do together with children as it offers so many learning opportunities, not just about nutrition but about care and respect for living things. Kids also get excited about eating their own produce.

I firmly believe every garden should have a lemon tree and preferably a lime as well. These work well in large planters or wine barrel halves if you have limited space. Of course if you do have the land, a fruit orchard and extensive vegetable garden would be the ideal!

Creative Condiments

Condiments, spreads and sauces are the perfect thing to transform your nutritious meals and snacks, making them taste delicious. They really can be the difference between a meal being a bit bland or truly satisfying.

You can use condiments creatively in lots of different ways, for example

- as dips with vegetables sticks or tapas-style meals
- as spreads on wraps or sandwiches
- dolloped onto your salad which gives a great textural difference
- added to the salad dressing
- mixed through pasta for an instant meal
- added into the sauce of your casserole or pie
- spread over a pizza base
- served on the side
- used as additional flavour in a slow cooked meal i.e. red wine vinaigrette added to a stew or coating a lamb roast with harissa.

The most common condiments which I make at home and recommend you start with, are **Bright Beet Hummus**, **Basil and Parsley Pesto**, **Nut Butter**, **Labneh**, **Harissa** and **Super Seven Sauce**.

Once a fortnight spend some creative time in your kitchen stocking up some of these staples so you can avoid having to purchase store-bought varieties.

Sensational Salads

As I've already mentioned, I highly recommend eating a salad entrée before every dinner. Year round they are a great nutrition boost that can be your best short cut to amazing health! Even when salad greens may be out of season, coleslaw and chunky mixed salads can be stunning.

Often people tell me they can't believe we have time as a busy young family to have an entrée as well as a main every night. What I've found, however, is it actually takes the pressure off at that busy time of night. It gives us something to eat even if the main still needs time to cook through.

By being flexible with our entrées and following the "simple food is best" French style of eating we can enjoy a variety of delicious salads, many of which take just 60 seconds or less to prepare, and none of them more than a few minutes. This can be done alongside setting the table. If you have children at home it offers them a great chance to get involved and help with the preparation.

Starting with your salad and making it fill your entire plate allows you to super-size your vegetable intake. You can still have other vegetables as part of your main dinner dish as well. Eating in this way makes it incredibly easy to ensure that at least half of your meal consists of colourful vegetables.

Dressing your salad with a tasty vinaigrette encourages you and your family to polish it off in one sitting so there won't be any waste. You also take the edge off your appetite by filling up on nutritious vegetables before starting on your main, thus slowing down the speed of your entire meal. This means you are much less likely to overeat.

In each of my meal plans I list an entrée before each main. Do note however that these are simply suggestions and idea starters. In practice I don't meal plan specific entrées for every meal. For me, this would add in more fuss and as you know I am all about keeping things simple and easy.

Rather than following a set recipe for my entrées, I tend to create new and different salads each night. I don't write entrées onto our displayed menu; I just simply know that we will have something to start with.

The only exception is if I want to remind myself of an ingredient to be used up or I have a certain dish in mind to accompany a meal.

Let's now look at how to make fantastic vinaigrettes and super simple salads. My sensational salad blueprints allow you to make endless salad entrées and even show you to how to turn them into complete meals.

Say hello to a diverse range of delicious salads your body and taste buds will love you for!

Great Vinaigrettes

Never eat a salad naked! It's boring and it just doesn't do it justice. Enjoy the flavour enhancement of a lovely vinaigrette with every salad. You can make your own dressing with just a handful of ingredients rather than a sugar, salt and preservative-laden, store-bought version.

Here is the classic fresh French vinaigrette recipe I learned while living in France:

- A grind of salt and pepper
- 1-2 tsp mustard
- 2 Tbsp red wine vinegar
- 3 Tbsp extra virgin olive oil

The traditional way to prepare this (which also saves on the washing up) is to mix your vinaigrette up directly in the bottom of your salad bowl before adding the salad ingredients.

1. Mix together the mustard, vinegar, salt and pepper until well combined.

Note that it is best to mix this before adding the oil as the vinegar helps the other ingredients combine properly.

2. Add the oil and mix well.

3. Add salad ingredients and turn it all together gently to coat everything evenly.

Vinaigrette in a Jar

What I recommend as a time saver however, is to mix up a larger quantity of vinaigrette in a jar to last you for a week or two. Simply store the jar in the fridge and shake it each time before serving. You can then pour or spoon out 2-4 tablespoons onto your salad, depending on the size, and mix it all well until everything is coated.

To make your classic vinaigrette in a jar simply combine:

- ½-1 tsp each salt and pepper
- 3-4 Tbsp mustard
- 2/3 cup acid
- 1 cup oil

The options are endless as you can use any sort of acid and any sort of oil in the ratio two parts acid to three parts oil. Varying the types of acids and oils you use will give you slightly different styles of vinaigrette. Try out different mustards or add in extra flavours such as honey or spices for even more variety.

real food less fuss 103

Try out any combination of the following:

Mustards – Dijon, wholegrain, English, or another condiment such as **Harissa** or **Nut Butter**

Acid – lemon juice, lime juice, malt vinegar, red wine vinegar, balsamic vinegar, raspberry vinegar, rice wine vinegar or apple cider vinegar.

Oil – extra virgin olive oil, macadamia oil, walnut oil, avocado oil, sesame oil, flaxseed oil or infused oils for extra flavour.

Vinaigrettes are easy to experiment with. So have fun and invent something new and unique each time! Here are some variations to try:

Sweet Citrus Dressing

- 3-4 Tbsp wholegrain mustard
- 2 Tbsp honey
- ⅓ cup lemon juice
- ⅓ cup orange juice
- ¾ cup olive oil
- ¼ cup lime infused olive oil
- ½-1 tsp each salt and pepper

Asian Style Dressing

- 2 tsp soy sauce
- 1 tsp oyster sauce
- 2/3 cup rice wine vinegar
- ¼ cup sesame oil
- ¾ cup olive oil
- 1 Tbsp garlic, crushed
- 2 Tbsp spring onions (scallions), sliced

Satay Dressing

- 4 Tbsp nut butter
- 2 Tbsp honey
- 2 Tbsp fresh ginger, diced
- ⅓ cup lemon juice
- ⅓ cup apple cider vinegar
- ⅓ cup olive oil

French Vinaigrette

- 3-4 Tbsp Dijon mustard
- ⅓ cup red wine vinegar
- ⅓ cup raspberry vinegar
- 1 cup oil
- 1 shallot, finely sliced
- ½-1 tsp each salt and pepper

Creamy Vinaigrette

- 3-4 Tbsp Dijon mustard
- 2/3 cup red wine vinegar
- 1 cup olive oil
- 4 Tbsp natural Greek yoghurt or Crème Fraîche
- ½-1 tsp each salt and pepper

North African Vinaigrette

- 3-4 Tbsp harrisa
- ⅔ cup balsamic vinegar
- ¾ cup olive oil
- ¼ cup sesame oil
- ½-1 tsp each salt and pepper

Sensational Salad Blueprints

Instant Salad Blueprint

Canned vegetables can be a lifesaver as an "instant" salad. In less than 60 seconds you can drain the juice, rinsing if required, then combine the contents with your pre-made classic vinaigrette and voila, it's done!

My favourites are

- lentils
- asparagus
- corn
- mixed beans
- beetroot (beets)
- chickpeas (garbanzo beans)

(or any combination of these).

Super Simple Salad Blueprint

These are a slight step up from the instant salad taking just a few minutes to prepare and are all simply delicious. They are some of the most common salads that my French family would routinely serve as their entrée.

Carrot Salad

Wash and grate three large carrots. Add the classic vinaigrette and mix well. Coriander (cilantro) and slivered almonds are a great addition to this as well.

Creamy Cucumber Salad

Slice a telegraph cucumber into very fine circular slices. Add the creamy vinaigrette and a good sprinkle of freshly cracked pepper and mix well.

Pink Beetroot Salad

Drain a can of sliced or diced beetroot (beets). Add the creamy vinaigrette and freshly diced herbs of your choice and mix well.

Green Salad

Wash and dry any lettuce greens. Add the classic vinaigrette and mix well. A few shallots finely sliced go especially well with this.

Tomato Salad

Wash and slice six large tomatoes into wedges. Add the classic vinaigrette and freshly diced parsley or basil and mix well.

Avocado Boats

Slice two ripe avocados lengthways, remove the stones. Squeeze over lemon juice, then salt and pepper. Serve straight onto your plate and eat with a teaspoon.

Lentil Salad

Drain and rinse a can of lentils. Dice a handful of parsley, slice one shallot and crush one clove of garlic. Combine everything together with your classic vinaigrette.

Chunky Mixed Salad Blueprint

I used to think that salad was always something with lettuce in it, but have found it quite freeing to realise the plethora of salads you can make without set rules. Not that I'm against lettuce – leafy greens are amazing! I just don't believe we need to be constrained to think that we can't make a salad without them.

As the name suggests chunky mixed salads have chunks of lots of different vegetables and flavour enhancers such as fruits, nuts and seeds. They are visually appealing, are packed with a wide range of minerals and nutrients and are great for using up whatever you have on hand. This step by step process will help you make countless salad combinations.

Salad Base — 1

Choose as many of these as you like.

- **Fresh vegetables** – carrot, capsicum (bell pepper), celery, tomato, cucumber, avocado, red onion, chilli
- **Extra vegetables if required** – use these if your fresh supplies are running low, you have leftover cooked vegetables on hand or you just want to add this flavour
  - **Canned vegetables** – corn, beans, lentils, beetroot (beets), chickpeas (garbanzo beans)
  - **Frozen vegetables** (defrosted) – peas, corn, beans
  - **Lightly cooked vegetables** – broccoli, cauliflower, asparagus, courgette (zucchini).

Note – you can also add any of these raw for extra crunch and even more goodness. Dice them up small or for the courgette try peeling them in long thin strips.

2 — Neutral, Sweet or Savoury

Decide if you are going to keep your salad neutral with the vegetables you have already chosen or turn it into something sweet or savoury. Choose one or more things from one list or the other.

- **Sweet** – apples, pears, grapes, oranges, pineapples, mango, nectarines, peaches, sultanas, dates, raisins, cranberries, figs
- **Savoury extras** – olives, sundried tomatoes, gherkins (pickles), mushrooms, capers, spring onions (scallions), pickled onions, shallots, finely diced or crushed garlic.

3 Extra Flavours

Choose one or more from any list to add to any salad. You may wish to brown the nuts or seeds in a hot dry pan for two to three minutes for an amazing flavour boost.

- **Nuts** – cashews, almonds, walnuts, macadamia nuts, pine nuts, Brazil nuts, pecans, hazelnuts
- **Seeds** – sunflower seeds, linseeds, pumpkin seeds (pepitas), chia seeds, black or white sesame seeds, cumin seeds
- **Cheeses** – edam cheese (cubed or grated), feta/goat's cheese, blue cheese, parmesan, labneh, haloumi
- **Fresh Herbs** – parsley, mint, coriander (cilantro), basil, chives, oregano
- **Sprouts** – mung bean, adzuki, alfalfa, blue pea, lentil sprouts.

4 Have a Great Vinaigrette

Every salad needs a delicious dressing. Add your favourite vinaigrette and combine it well so that everything is evenly coated. Match your vinaigrette to your salad by adding honey for sweet options, sesame oil for Asian style salads and balsamic vinegar or citrus juice for others depending on the flavours included. See the section on vinaigrettes for plenty of ideas.

5 Have Fun!

Enjoy experimenting with the endless variations of flavours and textures to see what you and your family most enjoy. You can even create variety with exactly the same ingredients by cutting them up differently, for example, peeling, grating, cutting lengthways, on an angle, into thick or thin slices, in different directions or into cubes. This visual and textural variety makes your salads all the more enjoyable.

Here are some of my favourite chunky mixed salad combinations to tempt your taste buds and give you ideas:

Neutral

- Diced carrot, cucumber and capsicum (bell pepper), cubed edam cheese, pumpkin seeds (pepitas) and mung beans
- Sliced tomato, carrot, celery, avocado and dollops of labneh
- Corn, kidney beans, diced carrot, almond flakes and parsley
- Broccoli florets, sliced capsicum (bell pepper) and tomato, crumbled feta cheese and basil
- Diced avocado and cucumber, pine nuts and grated parmesan

Sweet

- Sliced tomato, diced celery and apple, cubed edam cheese, sunflower seeds, parsley
- Diced cucumber, carrot and avocado, cashew nuts, raisins and chives
- Sliced carrot and pear, chopped walnuts, blue cheese and mint
- Diced beetroot (beets), cucumber and orange, diced feta cheese and mint
- Diced celery, capsicum (bell pepper) and carrots, grapes, walnuts and pumpkin seeds (pepitas)
- Sliced avocado, celery, mango and pineapple diced red onion and coriander (cilantro)
- Canned corn, chickpeas, (garbanzo beans) diced carrot and green beans, dates and parsley

Savoury

- Diced tomato, feta, red onion, sundried tomatoes and chilli, halved olives and basil
- Sliced beetroot (beets), tomato and shallots, diced garlic and parsley
- Canned chickpeas (garbanzo beans) and corn, halved cherry tomatoes, sliced mushrooms and grated parmesan
- Diced tomato, capsicum (bell pepper), cucumber, gherkins (pickles) and red onion
- Canned lentils, diced tomato, celery and spring onion (scallions) and parsley

Leafy Mixed Salad Blueprint

Leafy green vegetables are incredibly good for us and there are such a range of different types to choose from. They do however need to be looked after, stored well and eaten while very fresh for maximum flavour and goodness.

I highly recommend washing your greens and spinning them dry in a salad spinner before eating. Damp greens in a salad dilute the vinaigrette and really reduce the flavour. If you don't want to invest in a salad spinner, you can place them in a clean tea towel, hold the corners firmly and spin it outside. Just take care not to let your gorgeous greens go flying!

Leafy greens are delicious just on their own with a great dressing and they also pair well with any of the chunky mixed salad ideas above.

Simply select one or more types of leafy vegetables and add your chosen extras, as with the chunky mixed salad blueprint:

- Iceberg lettuce, cos lettuce, mesclun, baby spinach, silver beet (Swiss chard), red lettuce, curly lettuce, endives, white cabbage, red cabbage, savoy cabbage, watercress.

Some of my favourite combinations include:

- Mesclun, sliced sundried tomatoes, crumbled goat's cheese, diced chilli and pine nuts
- Torn cos lettuce, diced tomato, avocado and mango and chives
- Sliced iceberg lettuce, diced carrots, cucumber and celery, cubed edam cheese and sunflower seeds
- Finely sliced cabbage, grated carrot, sliced spring onion (scallion), sultanas, mint and sesame seeds
- Sliced endives and pear, crumbled blue cheese, walnuts and sunflower seeds
- Baby spinach, baby beets, halved cherry tomatoes, dollops of labneh, pumpkin seeds (pepitas), sliced almonds and parsley.

Make a Meal of It

To make more filling salads that make fabulous complete meals, add a carbohydrate and/or a protein option such as:

- **Carbohydrate** – pasta, rice, couscous, quinoa, croutons, boiled or roasted root vegetables.
- **Protein** – sliced chicken, roast beef, bacon pieces, diced ham, sliced lamb, tuna flakes, smoked or fresh salmon, anchovies, sardines, crab sticks, seafood, tofu, boiled or poached eggs.

Serve your salad hot, warm or cold according to your preference. With all of these options, you can create a never-ending list of great salads. The key is adding enough variety to make it interesting, balancing the flavours and tying it together with a great dressing.

Some of my favourite combinations include:

With Carbohydrate

- Roast vegetables, diced capsicum (bell pepper), cubed feta, sliced peaches and coriander (cilantro)
- Couscous, pumpkin (squash), peas, Brazil nuts and parsley
- Quinoa, diced tomatoes, capsicum (bell pepper) and cucumber, haloumi and mixed fresh herbs
- Rice, diced celery, carrot and cucumber, pineapple pieces, toasted cashew nuts, sultanas and chives

With Protein

- Tuna, mesclun, grated carrot, capsicum (bell pepper) strips and sunflower seeds
- Scallops, baby spinach, red onion
- Beef strips, mesclun, cherry tomatoes, courgette (zucchini) strips, julienne carrots
- Sliced lamb, baby spinach, sundried tomatoes, mint, basil and pine nuts
- Chicken, lettuce, sliced apricot, cranberries and sesame seeds
- Baby spinach, sliced avocado and poached eggs

With Protein and Carbohydrate

- Lamb, rice, baby spinach, orange, pumpkin seeds (pepitas), mint and dollops of labneh
- Pasta, tuna, tomato, steamed broccoli florets and parsley
- Quinoa, flaked salmon, sliced cucumber, capers and chives
- Potato, ham, eggs, mesclun, parsley and basil
- Chicken, cos lettuce, red onion, cucumber, poached eggs, crouton

Delicious with the Satay Dressing from pg 104

– PART VI –

Tying It All Together

An Ideal Week

Shopping Lists

Ensuring Success

An Ideal Week

Here are my ideal meal plans which have been crafted to tie together all of the principles discussed so far. I have included separate plans and the corresponding shopping lists for both a family of four to five people and for an individual, and I explain how they work and how to adapt them to cater to your family size and lifestyle.

Both meal plans give you a practical example of how to enjoy a balanced variety of meals that flow throughout your week, saving you time and fuss while maximising your nutrition. All of the recipes are included in the next section along with several bonus recipes which were just too good not to include. You can start from this base and continue planning endless weeks of meals ahead.

Enjoy!

Explanatory notes:

- In this example there are four meals already stored in the freezer at the start of the week. The numbers along the bottom represent how many frozen meals you have stored at the end of each day (in relation to what you've cooked and defrosted).

- Several of the meals flow onto a future meal, so refer to the notes at the bottom which explain the portions and meal ingredients to set aside. They also recommend when to bulk cook and freeze extra meals, when to make a batch of baking and when to soak your bircher muesli.

- The weekday breakfasts are quick and easy, while the weekend options include slightly more special breakfasts that take a little time to cook. (They are well worth the time!)

- Similarly the weekday lunches are quick and simple, made either of leftovers from dinner the night before or easy portable meals. The weekend lunches are great to share as a family or with friends.

- My suggested snacks include a mixture of home baking, smoothies, vegetables with condiments, or fresh fruit paired with either raw nuts or yoghurt. These are versatile suggestions which can be interchanged. This example assumes you have made a range of different recipes over the past few weeks and frozen them as ready snacks. If you don't have someone to share the smoothie with when you make it, save half of it in the fridge as a snack for the next day.

- The salad entrées are all just suggested ideas as well; feel free to switch them up as you see fit. The key is to use whatever produce you have on hand in relation to when it's fresh, following the sensational salad blueprints.

- While I haven't listed desserts on this meal plan, you might like to pick one or two evenings to enjoy a special treat. I have included some of my favourite dessert recipes for you as well.

- This meal plan and its corresponding shopping list are designed to suit families of four to five people. If you are catering for a bigger crowd you can of course make it stretch by increasing the recipes or simply make the triple portion for just two meals.

Family Meal Planner

Helping you eat more real food with less fuss!

Laura PARSONS — Wellbeing Specialists

real food *less fuss*

	Monday	Tuesday	Wednesday	Thursday	Friday	Saturday	Sunday
Breakfast	Quick Natural Muesli with Greek Yoghurt & Fresh Fruit	Bircher Muesli with Frozen Berries	Perfect Poached Eggs with Avo	Bircher Muesli with Sliced Banana	Quick Natural Muesli with Greek Yoghurt & Frozen Berries	Tasty Vegetarian Omelette	Golden Pumpkin Pancakes
Snack	Piece of Fresh Fruit with a Handful of Almonds	Green Vitality Smoothie	Vegetable Sticks with Bright Beet Hummus	Choc Nut Bliss Slice	Piece of Fresh Fruit with a Handful of Almonds	Orange Immunity Boosting Smoothie	Piece of Fresh Fruit with Greek Yoghurt
Lunch	Protein Packed Salad	Leftover Pork Roll	Tuna Salad For One	Leftover Coleslaw in a Wrap	Perfect Poached Eggs with Avo	Vibrant Quinoa Salad	Winter Warmer Soup
Snack	Celery Logs topped with Nut Butter	Beautiful Banana Biscuit	Ginger Fudge Slice	Piece of Fresh Fruit with Greek Yoghurt	Spinach, Feta and Mint Muffin	Vegetable Sticks with Bright Beet Hummus	Citrus Square
Entrée	Chunky Mixed Salad	Leafy Mixed Salad	Zesty Mint & Lime Coleslaw	Pink Beetroot Salad	Chunky Mixed Salad	Creamy Cucumber Salad	Avocado Boats
Dinner	Pork and Apple Rolls	Defrost a meal of choice	Simple Baked Salmon	Defrost a meal of choice	Salad Tacos with Best Beef Bolognaise	Succulent Lemon Roast Chicken	Defrost a meal of choice

Monday: Bulk cook the pork rolls. Save 1 portion for tomorrow's lunch & freeze 3 extra family dinners. Soak bircher muesli.

Tuesday: Relax!

Wednesday: Save some coleslaw (with the dressing separate) for lunch. Soak bircher muesli.

Thursday: Relax!

Friday: Bulk cook the best bolognaise and freeze 3 extra family size portions for future dinners.

Saturday: Set aside 1 cup of roasted pumpkin for breakfast. Make stock for the soup tomorrow.

Sunday: Make a batch of citrus squares and freeze most of them for the coming weeks. Freeze any leftover soup in portions as lunches.

Frozen Meals: 7 · 6 · 6 · 5 · 8 · 8 · 7

Imagine that you start this week with 4 meals in your freezer.

This is a great meal plan for solo cooks, which follows the same principles of the family meal plan. See the explanatory notes on **pg 118** as well as these notes:

- When you are cooking for one, you can enjoy even more nights off cooking all the while stocking your freezer. As you can see from the numbers along the bottom, you start with four frozen meals on hand and finish up with 10, so this example sets you up for even easier weeks ahead.
- If you are cooking for two you can simple double up the recipes and follow a very similar plan, you just won't have so many extra frozen meals at the end of the week.
- Some of the snacks and meals are repeated over two days to save you time.
  - You can make the smoothies as a double portion and set one aside in the fridge for the following day.
  - Salads such as the coleslaw and beetroot (beets) salads can be used over multiple days.
  - The vegetarian omelette can be cooked with half of it saved and reheated in the pan on Sunday. Or, you can prep and dice the vegetables and set half of them aside in the fridge, then simply whisk through the eggs and cook your fresh omelette the next day.
- This meal plan assumes that you have previously done a variety of baking so you have a mixture of different snacks already in the freezer. The bulk baking and cooking day on the weekend would only need to be done once every two or three weeks to keep your freezer stocked.
- As always, refer to the notes below each day which explain the portions and meal ingredients to set aside to flow to the next meal.
- Being a solo cook, you will need to invest in a good set of freezer containers. Also labelling and dating everything becomes even more important as you will be making several more portions each time you cook in bulk and will want to ensure you rotate through your library of meals and baking regularly.

Go to www.realfoodlessfuss.com/resources to receive this and other printable meal planning resources.

Individual Meal Planner

realfood less fuss

Helping you eat more real food with less fuss!

	Monday	Tuesday	Wednesday	Thursday	Friday	Saturday	Sunday
Breakfast	Quick Natural Muesli with Greek Yoghurt & Fresh Fruit	Bircher Muesli with Frozen Berries	Perfect Poached Eggs with Avo	Bircher Muesli with Sliced Banana	Quick Natural Muesli with Greek Yoghurt & Frozen Berries	Tasty Vegetarian Omelette	Tasty Vegetarian Omelette
Snack	Piece of Fresh Fruit with a Handful of Almonds	Green Vitality Smoothie	Green Vitality Smoothie	Choc Nut Bliss Slice	Orange Immunity Boosting Smoothie	Orange Immunity Boosting Smoothie	Celery Logs topped with Nut Butter
Lunch	Tuna Salad For One	Leftover Pork Roll	Leftover Coleslaw in a Wrap	Protein Packed Salad	Leftover Portion from Last Night	Tuna Salad For One	Best Beef Bolognaise and Salad Wrap
Snack	Celery Logs topped with Nut Butter	Beautiful Banana Biscuit	Ginger Fudge Slice	Piece of Fresh Fruit with Greek Yoghurt	Spinach, Feta and Mint Muffin	Piece of Fresh Fruit with a Handful of Almonds	Citrus Square
Entrée	Zesty Mint & Lime Coleslaw	Zesty Mint & Lime Coleslaw	Leafy Mixed Salad	Pink Beetroot Salad	Pink Beetroot Salad	Avocado Boat	Avocado Boat
Dinner	Pork and Apple Roll	Defrost a meal of choice	Defrost a meal of choice	Defrost a meal of choice	Salad Tacos with Best Beef Bolognaise	Spaghetti Bolognaise	Ratatouille Pizza

Frozen Meals: 8 | 7 | 6 | 5 | 9 | 9 | 10

Imagine that you start this week with 4 meals in your freezer

Cook a half batch of pork rolls. Save 1 portion for tomorrow's lunch & freeze 4 dinners. Save 2 servings of the coleslaw with dressing on the side. Soak bircher muesli.

Relax!

Soak bircher muesli.

Defrost 2 frozen portions and set one aside for tomorrow's lunch. Save half of the beetroot salad for tomorrow's entrée.

Bulk cook the beef bolognaise and set aside 2 portions in the fridge for this weekend. Freeze 5 extra portions.

Relax!

Make the pizza using 1 eggplant and save half for tomorrow's lunch. Freeze the left over sauce for a future meal. Make a batch of citrus slice and freeze it for the coming weeks.

real food less fuss

Shopping lists

Recommended Staples

The following is a list of the general staple items I recommend you have on hand at all times; for example to make up muesli and vinaigrettes and for snacks. To avoid repetition, I don't name these standard pantry items in the other shopping lists.

Pantry Staples

Whole oats and quick oats

Bran sticks

LSA (ground linseed, sunflower, almond)

Sultanas or raisins and dates

Red wine, balsalmic, apple cider and white vinegar

Extra virgin olive oil

Coconut oil

Honey, maple syrup

Vanilla extract

Cacao or cocoa powder

Wholemeal flour

Baking powder and soda

Cornflour or arrowroot

Herbal teas

Dry herbs and spices, salt and pepper

Almonds, cashews, Brazil nuts

Sunflower, pumpkin (pepitas), chia and sesame seeds

Quinoa

Brown rice

Wholemeal pasta and couscous

Fridge

Greek natural yoghurt

Wholegrain and Dijon mustard

Milk

Butter

Tasty or edam and parmesan cheese

Pickles and olives

Dessicated coconut

Freezer

Frozen berries

Frozen peas, corn, beans

Homemade liquid stock

Frozen lemon and lime juice and zest

Diced ginger

Fresh Produce

A mixture of salad vegetables for mixed salads

Fresh herbs (In the garden or pots is great)

Fresh fruit for snacks

Family Shopping List

Meat & Seafood

4 200g (7oz) salmon fillets

750g (1.5lb) mince beef

1 medium free range chicken

1kg (2lbs) pork mince

Vegetables

12 potatoes

½ pumpkin (squash)

12 carrots

2 garlic bulbs

5 onions

1 red onion

3 spring onions

1 packet baby spinach

2 cos lettuce (romaine)

½ cabbage

1 broccoli

2 courgettes (zucchini)

1 leek

1 celery

4 tomatoes

6 mushrooms

1-2 chillis

sprouts

2 bunches parsley

2 handfuls mint

Dry & Packaged Goods

1 95g (3oz) can of tuna of your choice

1 400g (14oz) can chickpeas (garbanzo beans)

2 400g (14oz) can sliced beetroot (beets)

1 400g (14oz) can corn kernels

1 400g (14oz) can red kidney beans

3 400g (14oz) cans diced tomatoes

1 cup dry red lentils

½ cup tomato paste

8 wholemeal wraps

2 dozen eggs

Fruit

2 bananas

1 kiwifruit

2 oranges

2 apples

4 avocados

6 lemons

2 limes

Plus fresh fruit of your choice for snacks

Individual Shopping List

Meat
750g (1.5lb) mince beef
500g (1lb) pork mince

Vegetables
6 carrots
1 garlic bulb
4 onions
1 red onion
1 packet baby spinach
1 cos lettuce (romaine)
½ cabbage
1 capsicum (bell pepper)
3 courgettes (zucchini)
1 eggplant (aubergine)
½ a celery
12 cherry tomatoes
8 mushrooms
sprouts
1 bunch parsley
2 handfuls mint

Dry & Packaged Goods
2 95g (3oz) cans of tuna of your choice
1 400g (14oz) can sliced beetroot (beets)
4 400g (14oz) cans diced tomatoes
1 cup dry red lentils
5 wholemeal wraps
1 dozen eggs

Fruit
2 bananas
1 kiwifruit
2 oranges
1 apple
3 avocados
4 lemons
1 lime
Plus fresh fruit of your choice for snacks

Ensuring Success

Here is a final overview of the key principles that will make meal planning work for you. Before you know it, they will become ingrained as a mindset which will transform not only your pantry but your entire life.

- Once a week plan your meals for the week ahead to suit your lifestyle.
- Feel flexible to change your meal plan as other plans change throughout your week. (Just make sure you come up with a nutritious plan B!)
- Suit your plan to what is seasonally available and select whatever fresh produce that appeals to base your salads on.
- Keep up the "zero food waste" mentality by making the most of leftovers and by treating recipes as a guide, allowing you to substitute in whatever is on hand to be used up.
- Save yourself time by shortcutting future meals to flow from one to another and by doing your *mise en place* preparation and your cooking in bulk whenever possible.
- Remember to set aside the intended extra portions for lunch and/or to freeze before serving your meal. The before part is very important!
- Label and date everything you freeze and rotate meals through your "freezer-library".
- Put on your favourite music and enjoy a weekend of batch cooking, making condiments, sauces, baking and complete meals.
- Most of all have fun with it. Stay organised yet flexible about how things turn out and enjoy just how much this mindset simplifies and improves your life!

– PART VII –

Recipes

Breakfasts pg 130-141

Quick Natural Muesli
Bircher Muesli
Tasty Vegetarian Omelette
Wholesome Homemade Bread
Perfect Poached Eggs with Avo
Golden Pumpkin Pancakes

Light Meals pg 142-155

Protein Packed Salad
Tuna Salad for One
Vibrant Quinoa Salad
Roast Veggie Salad
Blue Cheese and Pear Salad
Zesty Lime and Mint Coleslaw
Winter Warmer Soup
Creamy Pork Bone and Pumpkin Soup

Dinners pg 156-175

Risotto That Cooks Itself
Salad Tacos with Best Beef Bolognaise
Pork and Apple Rolls
Ratatouille Pizza
Moroccan Lamb and Mint Meatballs
4C Creamy Coconut Chicken Casserole
Easy Kumara and Lentil Dhal
Succulent Lemon Roast Chicken
French Lamb and Date Tajine
Simple Baked Salmon

Desserts pg 176-187

Naturally Good Chocolate Brownie
Unbelievably Good Ice Cream
Perfect Pumpkin Pie
Secret Chocolate Mousse
Banoffee Pie
Lemon Lime Pistachio Cheesecakes

Drinks pg 202-209

Immunity Boosting Smoothie
Green Vitality Smoothie
Hot Lemon and Ginger
Authentic Spiced Chai Latte

Condiments, Sauces & Flavour Enhancers pg 188-201

Super Seven Sauce
Bright Beet Hummus
Parsley and Basil Pesto
Harissa
Labneh
Nut Butter
Date Puree
Stewed Apple

Snacks pg 210-221

Beautiful Banana Biscuits
Choc Nut Bliss Slice
Spinach, Feta and Mint Muffins
Citrus Squares
Quinoa Quiche
Ginger Fudge Slice

Quick Natural Muesli

This simple recipe is so filling and nutritious. It has lots of wholegrains and healthy fats which give you long lasting energy to curb cravings, as well as fibre to assist digestion. As it is a natural muesli it is super easy and quick to mix up whenever you run out.

PREP TIME

- 1kg (2lb) wholegrain rolled oats
- 500g (1lb) regular rolled oats
- 500g (1lb) all bran
- 1 cup desiccated coconut
- 1 cup LSA (ground linseed, sunflower and almonds)
- ½ cup white or black chia seeds
- 1 cup of dried fruit such as sultanas or diced dates (optional)

Note – Oats are considered low gluten. They do contain the avenin form of gluten which is fine for some, but not all, people with gluten intolerance. Some people find a soaked bircher muesli is better for their digestion.

1. Combine all the ingredients in a large bowl and store in an airtight container.
2. Serve with milk, Greek yoghurt and fresh fruit, such as raspberries, kiwifruit or banana.

Variations:

Leave out the dried fruit for a lower sugar version.

Leave out the bran for a wheat free, low gluten version.

To make it extra special, add a little cinnamon or vanilla essence to taste.

Quick Tip – keep a 1/2 cup measure in the container rather than pouring it out to help keep the serving size consistent.

Bircher Muesli

Not only is bircher muesli delicious, pre-soaking the grains and seeds enhances their nutritional offering and makes them more easily digested. So you get even more goodness out of them without any digestive discomfort. This is my staple weekday breakfast and is incredibly convenient being ready to take straight out of the fridge and enjoy. I hope you love it as much as I do!

PREP TIME

Dry Ingredients

1kg (2lb) **wholegrain oats**

1 cup **LSA** (ground linseed, sunflower and almonds)

1 cup **desiccated coconut**

1 cup **sunflower** or **pumpkin seeds** (pepitas)

2 tsp **cinnamon** (if desired)

To Serve

Approx. ½ cup **milk**

3 Tbsp **blueberries**

1. Combine the dry muesli ingredients in a large bowl and store in an airtight container.

2. In the evening scoop out ½ a cup of the muesli into a bowl and cover it with milk and top with blueberries. (Either fresh or frozen are fine, they will defrost overnight.)

3. In the morning add extra milk to get it to your desired consistency. Enjoy!

Variations:

Add a dollop of Greek yoghurt for a thicker creamier version.

*For a dairy free version use coconut milk or another dairy free alternative.

To boost fibre content add 2 tablespoons psyllium husk.

Tasty Vegetarian Omelette

This makes a scrumptious weekend breakfast, brunch or lunch (or even an easy dinner.) The spectrum of bright colourful vegetables mean you are getting a wide range of vitamins, minerals and antioxidants. The eggs offer a complete form of protein as well as healthy fats which assist with the absorption of vitamins A, D, E and K. Combined with the fibre from all of the vegetables this meal sets you up for sustained high energy throughout the day.

SERVES   TOTAL TIME

- 1 Tbsp **butter**
- ¼ of a **red onion**, diced
- 6 **mushrooms**, diced
- 1 **carrot**, finely grated
- 8 **eggs**
- 1 cup **tasty cheese**, grated
- 1 bunch **parsley**, diced

Note – Feel free to substitute any of the vegetables for what you have on hand. This is a great little meal to use up leftovers including cooked vegetables from the previous night's dinner. Just dice them up small, or if you are running low on fresh produce opt for frozen peas, canned corn or mushrooms.

1. Heat a large non-stick fry pan with the butter. Dice and cook the vegetables for 3-4 minutes with the lid on until softened, then lower heat to medium.

2. Meanwhile in a small bowl, beat the eggs together with the grated cheese and diced parsley.

3. Add the egg mixture to the pan and stir for a few seconds so the egg gets through to the bottom and everything is evenly combined. Leave it to cook gently for 3-4 minutes.

4. Flip the omelette. It is easiest to slice the omelette quarters and flip it one section at a time. Allow the other side to cook through for a further 1-2 minutes. Serve while hot.

Wholesome Homemade Bread

This bread is an adaptation of a recipe from a friend Louise. It requires no kneading and can easily be mixed up in a few minutes, then left until baking time. It makes a lovely textured loaf with a gorgeous crust and works well both served fresh and as toast. As there aren't any preservatives in the bread it will go stale much more quickly than most store bought varieties, so slice and freeze what you won't use that day and defrost it at your leisure.

MAKES 2   PREP TIME 5   COOK TIME 1 HR   DF   V

1 tsp **salt**
3 cups (750ml, 25fl oz) **lukewarm water**
1 tsp **dried yeast**
350g (12.5oz) **wholemeal flour**
300g (10.5oz) **plain flour**
½ cup (45g, 1.5oz) **oats**
½ cup (85g, 3oz) **sunflower seeds**
½ cup (85g, 3oz) **pumpkin seeds** (pepitas)
3 Tbsp **chia seeds**

1. Sit a large mixing bowl on top of your kitchen scales and tare it to zero. Add the salt, water and then yeast. (The yeast will float on top of the water keeping it away from the salt which can inhibit its action.)

2. Tare the scales to zero again and add the flour, oats and seeds, reserving 1 Tbsp of the chia seeds.

3. Mix all of the ingredients together until it resembles a moist cake mixture.

4. Scrape it out into two well-greased, high sided loaf tins. Smooth out the mixture and sprinkle the remaining chia seeds on top.

5. Cover the tins with plastic bags puffed up like chefs hats and leave them in a warm place for 12-24 hours while the mix rises up to the top of the tin. In warmer weather 12 hours will generally be enough time, in cooler weather they may take longer to rise.

6. Preheat the oven to 200°C (390°F) and bake both loaves in the centre of the oven for 1 hour or until the bases sound hollow when tapped. You may need to cover the tins loosely with aluminium for the final 10-15 minutes if they are browning up too fast.

7. The loaves are easiest to slice when cooled, but are of course delicious fresh from the oven!

Perfect Poached Eggs with Avo

It took me years to figure out how to perfectly poach an egg. It used to be something I only ever ordered at restaurants, but now I know how to turn them out at home. The secret lies in adding vinegar to the water and having it at the correct temperature before adding the eggs. Eggs are a complete form of protein and combined with the fibre and goodness in the grainy toast and the leafy greens, this meal really satisfies.

SERVES   PREP TIME

- 2 free range **eggs**
- 2-3 Tbsp **white vinegar**
- 1-2 slices **wholesome homemade bread** (pg 136)
- ¼ of a ripe **avocado**
- A handful of **baby spinach**
- **Salt** and **pepper**

Variations:

Substitute the avocado for pan fried tomatoes if desired.

Add smoked salmon and serve with half a lemon squeezed over the top.

1. Bring a saucepan or frying pan of 4 cm (approx 1.5 inches) deep water to the boil along with the vinegar.

2. Once it is at a good strong boil, turn the temperature down to medium and immediately crack your eggs in quickly but gently by holding them close to the water.

3. Put the lid half on and keep the water at a very gentle steady simmer for 2-3 minutes for runny yolks, or 4-6 minutes if you prefer them well done.

4. Meanwhile, cook the toast and top it with sliced avocado and baby spinach leaves. Remove eggs with a sieved spoon and a clean tea towel to gently pat them dry. Place the eggs on top and season with fresh cracked pepper and enjoy while hot!

Golden Pumpkin Pancakes

Children and adults alike will love these gorgeous golden mini pancakes. They are great for breakfast, brunch or as an afternoon snack. They also freeze well so are perfect to cook in bulk and save leftovers for lunchboxes. The pumpkin is a rich source of vitamin A, phytochemicals and fibre. The cinnamon is a wonderful antioxidant, anti-inflammatory and it helps to stabilise blood sugar levels.

SERVES 4   PREP TIME 5   COOK TIME 10

- 1 cup roasted pumpkin (squash)
- 1 egg
- 1 tsp vanilla extract
- 3 Tbsp pure maple syrup
- 1 cup milk
- ½ cup rolled oats
- 1 cup wholemeal flour
- 1 tsp baking powder
- 1 tsp cinnamon
- A pinch of salt

1. Mash the pumpkin with a fork and combine with all wet ingredients in a bowl.

2. Add all the dry ingredients and combine everything gently. It should be a moist mixture you can almost pour. If too thin add more flour, if too thick add more milk or water.

3. Heat a non-stick fry pan on a medium heat and melt a small knob of butter or coconut oil.

4. Spoon out generous spoonfuls to make several mini pancakes. Cook to golden brown on both sides. Keep pancakes warm in the oven while you cook remaining batches.

5. Serve topped with fresh fruit or berries, almond flakes, Greek yoghurt and a little maple syrup if desired.

Mason Jar Salads

Mason jars are an easy way to prepare a delicious nutritious lunch to take with you out and about. The trick is to layer them keeping the leafy greens away from the dressing. Start by mixing your dressing in the bottom of the jar – ½ tsp **mustard**, 2 tsp **red wine vinegar**, 1 Tbsp **olive oil**, **salt** and **pepper**. Or simply use your pre-made vinaigrette in a jar. Layer over the chunky vegetables that will withstand a little soaking and top it off with your greens. Once you shake it out onto a plate or bowl the dressing will coat everything and it will look amazing.

Protein Packed Salad

Protein from the eggs, almonds and cheese provides the essential building blocks to repair and rebuild cells. The sprouts, being a kernel of life, are a nutritional powerhouse and the mixture of textures and colours in this salad are not only delicious but provide you with vital nutrients, making this salad a wonderful anti-ageing combination.

SERVES 1   PREP TIME 10   GF   V

- 2 **eggs**, hard boiled
- 30g (1oz) **cheese**, cubed
- 10-12 **raw almonds**
- 6-8 **olives**
- ¼ cup **corn**
- ¼ cup **sprouts**
- 2 handfuls **mixed salad greens**

1. Boil eggs by placing them in cold or lukewarm water. Bring it to the boil, then simmer gently for 4-5 minutes.

2. Cube the cheese and shell the eggs under running cold water then slice into halves.

3. Add the dressing, and other ingredients to the jar leaving the salad greens till last.

Tuna Salad for One

Tuna contains essential omega-3 fatty acids which support vital brain and body functions. Together with the colourful vegetables and seeds, this salad offers a wide range of antioxidants.

SERVES 1 PREP TIME 5   GF   DF

1 **gherkin** (pickle)

1 small **carrot,**

6 **cherry tomatoes**, or 1 **tomato**

1 95g (3oz) can of **tuna** of your choice

1 Tbsp **pumpkin seeds** (pepitas)

2 handfuls of **baby spinach**

1. Roughly dice the gherkin and carrot and halve the tomatoes.

2. Add the dressing and chunky vegetables to your jar. Top with the tuna, seeds and baby spinach and some sliced lemon if desired.

Vibrant Quinoa Salad

This gorgeous salad is packed with goodness and fibre and is very low GI giving you lasting energy. Quinoa is similar to a grain with a lovely subtle nutty flavour. It is a complete protein being one of the few vegetable sources of all nine essential amino acids (building blocks for the body.) A good serving of this salad makes for a complete meal and leftovers make a tasty lunch the next day! This recipe serves four people as a main or eight as an entrée or side salad.

SERVES PREP TIME

1 cup **quinoa**

3 **spring onions**, diced

1 400g (14oz) can **corn kernels**

1 400g (14oz) can **red kidney beans**, drained and rinsed

½ a **cucumber**, sliced lengthways in quarters then diced into chunks

90g (3oz) **tasty cheese**, cubed

1 red **chilli**, deseeded and finely diced (optional)

Dressing

4 Tbsp **olive oil**

Zest and juice of 1 **lime** (or lemon)

1 tsp **honey**

Salt and **pepper** to season

1. Rinse quinoa well in a large sieve (this is important to remove any bitter taste), then bring to the boil in 2 cups of salted water and simmer for 15 minutes until all the water is absorbed. Once it is cooked the little white tails will show. Leave it to sit for 5 minutes then transfer it to a large bowl, fluff it up with a fork and allow it to cool.

2. While the quinoa simmers prepare all the other ingredients and mix the dressing up in a small bowl.

3. Combine everything together with the dressing and mix until it is all evenly coated. Taste and check the seasoning. Serve either warm or chilled.

Variation:

*Omit cheese for a dairy free option.

Roast Veggie Salad

This colourful salad is delicious, full of goodness and makes a satisfying lunch, entrée or main. The roast vegetables add a beautiful caramelised flavour and the vinaigrette really ties it all together. Super simple to do, you can save yourself time by pre-roasting the veggies along with dinner the day before. You can even top it with poached eggs, grilled chicken or beef strips to make a complete meal of it.

SERVES 4   PREP TIME 10   COOK TIME 30   GF   DF   V

2 **capsicums** (bell pepper), 1 red, 1 yellow

2 **carrots**

1 **brown onion**

4 large handfuls **spinach leaves**

8 cherry **tomatoes**

1 bunch **parsley**

Vinaigrette

1 tsp **wholegrain mustard**

1 Tbsp **balsamic vinegar**

1 Tbsp **lemon juice**

3 Tbsp **olive oil**

Salt and **pepper**

1. Slice capsicums, carrots and onion into similar sizes. Roast them at 180°C (360 °F) with a glug of oil, stirring occasionally for 25-30 minutes until golden and caramelised.

2. Mix together the mustard, vinegar and lemon juice in a small bowl. Then add the oil and seasoning and stir until well combined.

3. Halve the cherry tomatoes and dice the parsley.

4. Combine everything and gently stir until all of the leaves are coated in the vinaigrette. Serve either warm or chilled.

Go to www.bit.ly/CWLRoastVegeSalad for a step by step demonstration video.

Blue Cheese and Pear Salad

Blue cheese pairs beautifully with pears and walnuts. This sophisticated salad is deceptively easy, which makes it perfect as an entrée for dinner parties. You can prep all of the components in advance and combine it at the last minute. The leafy greens and pears are packed with antioxidants and fibre; and the walnuts and oils add healthy fats which are great for your skin, hair and brain.

SERVES PREP TIME

4 large handfuls **mixed salad greens** or **baby kale**

2 **pears**

120g (4oz) **blue vein cheese**

30g (1oz) **walnuts**

Vinaigrette

1 tsp **Dijon mustard**

2 Tbsp **apple cider vinegar**

3 Tbsp **olive oil**

Salt and **pepper**

1. In a small bowl mix up the vinaigrette adding the oil last.

2. In a wide salad bowl toss the greens together with the vinaigrette until everything is well coated.

3. Slice the pears and dice the cheese. Mix half through the greens and dot the remainder on top along with the walnuts. Serve immediately.

Note – This salad goes well with croutons. Simply slice some of your wholesome wholemeal bread into half-inch sized squares. Pan fry them with a little oil and a pinch of salt, stirring occasionally for 3-4 minutes until crispy and golden.

Zesty Lime and Mint Coleslaw

Cabbage is full of vitamins, minerals and fibre that help you look and feel amazing. Finding interesting ways to serve it raw means you get maximum goodness out of it. This coleslaw is delicious with the fresh flavour of the mint and the zesty lime, along with the nutty flavours of the toasted nuts and seeds. These also contribute healthy essential oils along with the olive oil. It makes a great entrée or a side dish which goes especially well with beef or pork.

SERVES 4-6   PREP TIME 10   GF   DF   V

- ¼ cup **sliced almonds**
- 3 Tbsp **sesame seeds**
- ⅓ **cabbage**, very finely sliced
- ¼ of a **red onion**, diced
- 2 handfuls **mint**, chopped

Dressing

- 1 **lime**, zest and juice
- 4 Tbsp **extra virgin olive oil**
- 1 Tbsp **honey** (optional)
- **Salt** and **pepper**

1. Brown the almonds and seeds in a fry pan on high. This only takes 2-3 minutes, so take care and watch them closely so as not to over cook them! Tip them into a bowl to cool.

2. Roughly chop the mint. Finely chop the onion and the cabbage with a very sharp knife. Thin crunchy cabbage is essential for the mouth feel of this salad, so chunk the cabbage into workable pieces before you start to ensure you get nice thin slices.

3. Zest then juice the lime and combine the dressing in a large salad bowl. Add all the other ingredients and mix together well. Serve immediately.

Variation:

Use the Satay Vinagrette from **pg 104** for a delicious Asian style flavour.

Winter Warmer Soup

After serving a roast chicken I always make stock and often this delicious soup. It is quick and simple to throw together, then leave to simmer. Feel free to vary the vegetables according to what you have on hand.

SERVES PREP TIME COOK TIME

1 **leek**, sliced
4 cloves, **garlic**, crushed
2 **carrots**, sliced
2 **potatoes**, sliced
1 bunch **parsley**, chopped
10 cups **stock** (as below)
Salt and **pepper**

1. In a soup pot, soften the leek and garlic with a little oil for 5 minutes, while you slice the other vegetables and chop the parsley.

2. Add the remaining ingredients and cook until tender.

3. Taste and season with salt and pepper as desired. Serve either chunky as it is, or mix with a stick blender for a smooth thick soup as pictured.

Chicken Stock

What could be better than a wholesome homemade stock? It is a fantastic base for soups, casseroles and risottos. A small amount can also be used to deglaze a pan, after browning onions for example. Try this out next time you serve a roast chicken and feel free to add any extra vegetables that need to be used up.

1 **chicken carcass**
1 **carrot**, chopped into chunks
1 **onion**, halved
2 **bay leaves**
Salt and **pepper**

1. Place the ingredients in a large saucepan and cover with approximately 3 litres (6 pints) of water. Simmer gently for 2 or more hours.

2. Strain the stock through a sieve and discard the carcass and bones. Store any stock you will use within 2 days in the fridge and freeze the rest.

Creamy Pork Bone and Pumpkin Soup

My husband and I created this soup for a mid-winter Christmas dinner we hosted when my youngest daughter was just a few weeks old. It's an incredibly easy entrée to make ahead of time and is perfect for entertaining (or simply to enjoy as a family on a cold day). Full of antioxidants, vitamins and minerals this soup has stunning colour and a rich thick texture. I love the balance of creaminess from the coconut milk and the punch of flavour from the pork bone and ginger.

SERVES PREP TIME COOK TIME

- 1-2 **pork bones**
- 1-2 **celery stalks** or **celery tops**
- 1 large 2kg (4lb) **pumpkin** (squash)
- 2 400ml (14fl oz) cans **coconut milk**
- 4 Tbsp fresh **ginger**, finely diced
- **Salt** and **pepper**

1. In a large stock pot or slow cooker simmer the pork bone with the celery stalks or tops, covered with about 6 cups (3 pints) of water for 2 or more hours. Then strain out the bones and other items, leaving a lovely flavoursome stock as a base for your soup.

2. Meanwhile cut the pumpkin into large chunks (or use pre-cut pieces to avoid chopping) and place it in a roasting pan. Roast at 180°C (360°F) for 40 minutes.

3. Once the pumpkin flesh is soft, remove from the oven and allow it to cool enough to work with. Scoop out the flesh and add to the stock along with the coconut milk, ginger and seasoning.

4. Simmer gently for 20 minutes to allow the flavours to combine. Blend with a stick blender for a perfectly smooth soup or mash with a potato masher for a slightly textured one.

5. Taste and adjust the seasoning. Serve hot with fresh coriander or parsley. Any leftovers can be kept in the fridge for two days or will freeze well. You might like to freeze individual portions for lunch and family sized portions for future dinners.

Variations:

For more punch add fresh chilli or chilli flakes to taste.

*Omit the pork bone and use a vegetable stock for a vegetarian version.

Risotto That Cooks Itself

This is the ultimate lazy risotto that doesn't require any stirring! Ridiculously easy and delicious, you really can't go wrong with this recipe. Simply assemble the ingredients and leave it to cook. If you have homemade stock in the freezer it's a wonderful way to put this to use, or a quality store bought variety will work fine. It's fabulous for using up leftovers. The recipe is very forgiving so you can add things in or change things around as long as you have the rice and stock in proportion.

SERVES   PREP TIME   COOK TIME

1 cup **rice** (preferably Arborio)

2½ cups of **liquid stock**

2 Tbsp **butter**

650g (1½lb) **pumpkin** (squash), peeled and diced

150g (5oz) quality **bacon**, roughly diced

½ cup **parmesan cheese**, grated

A handful of fresh **basil** to serve

Salt and **pepper**

1. Preheat oven to 190°C (375°F). Place rice, stock, butter, pumpkin and bacon in an oven proof dish and season with a good grind of salt and pepper.

2. Bake covered for 30 minutes, or until rice is soft.

3. Stir through half the parmesan, and serve with the remaining parmesan as a garnish, along with a liberal serve of basil leaves.

Salad Tacos with Best Beef Bolognaise

American friends Jessica and Dan first introduced us to this delicious way to eat "tacos". Combined with this tasty bolognaise, they are a fantastic family meal as children can enjoy choosing their own fillings. The lettuce leaves add a fresh crunch and make them much easier to eat; no more cracked taco shells falling apart! The bolognaise freezes well to use later on in cottage pies, pasta bakes, with spaghetti, in lasagne, as a pizza topping or in wraps. The lentils are an economical way to make this meal go further, plus they add lots of protein and fibre making it really filling.

SERVES 8+   PREP TIME 15   COOK TIME 20   GF DF V*

Best Beef Bolognaise

2 **onions**

4 cloves **garlic**, crushed or diced

750g (1.5lb) **mince beef**

2 **carrots**, grated

2 **courgettes** (zucchini), grated

1 bunch **parsley**, chopped

3 400g (14oz) cans **diced tomatoes**

1 cup **dry red lentils**

½ cup **tomato paste**

Salt and **pepper**

To serve as Tacos

2-3 **cos lettuce** (romaine)

Fillings as desired such as **tomatoes**, **cucumber**, **carrot**, **chilli**, **olives**, **cheese**, **avocado**

Optional extra sauces such as **harissa**, **pesto**, **labneh**

1. Soften onion and garlic in a fry pan with a little oil for 2-3 minutes. Then add the mince to brown for another 2-3 minutes.

2. Meanwhile grate the carrots and zucchini and chop the parsley. A time saving way to grate lots of vegetables at once is by using the grating blade attachment of your food processor.

3. Add the remaining bolognaise ingredients and simmer for 12-15 minutes allowing the sauce to reduce and the lentils to cook till tender.

4. Meanwhile, wash and dry the lettuce and prepare your toppings, placing them in small bowls.

5. Serve tacos by filling each lettuce leaf with your favourite combination of vegetables, cheese, bolognaise and sauces.

Pork and Apple Rolls

These are a firm family favourite in our household and are adapted from a recipe my friend Tess shared with me many years ago. Much more than your average sausage roll, they are packed with extra fibre and nutrients from the vegetables and apple, and rather than puff pastry, the wraps make for a healthier option that really does work! These freeze well so I always tend to make several at once.

SERVES PREP TIME COOK TIME

1kg (2lbs) **pork mince**

2 large **onions**, finely diced

2 **green apples**, grated (skin on)

3 **carrots**, grated

1½ cups **rolled oats**

2 tsp **cinnamon** (optional)

1 tsp **salt** and a grind of **pepper**

3 **eggs** beaten, plus 1 **egg** for brushing

4-6 **wholemeal wraps**

1. Preheat oven to 180°C (360°F). Dice the onion and grate the apple and carrot. (You can use the grater attachment of your food processor to speed this up.)

2. Combine everything apart from the wraps and one of the eggs in a large bowl. Beat the other egg in a small bowl.

3. On lined oven trays, divide the mixture into log shapes along the centre of each wrap. Make sure the edges can overlap at the top. Square wraps are ideal for this, but round ones work just as well if you trim off two edges. In this case make 6 shorter rolls instead of 4.

4. Close the wraps, overlapping and sticking them down by painting the beaten egg on with a pastry brush. Brush the remaining egg mixture all over the wraps to give a lovely colour when baked. Bake for 30 minutes until golden brown.

Notes:

When freezing extra portions it's best to slightly undercook the spare rolls by removing them 5-10 minutes early so that when you reheat at a later date they can crisp up in the oven without burning.

This mixture also works a treat as a meatloaf or meatballs. You could make all three versions at once from the same mixture, stocking your freezer with a variety of options.

This meal pairs well with roasted vegetables like these homemade kumara (sweet potato) wedges and roasted Brussel sprouts. Give the kumara the full cook time and add the sprouts (salted along with a knob of butter) for the final 10 minutes. Delicious!

Ratatouille Pizza

This is an incredibly quick and simple way to serve a flavoursome pizza without the additives store bought varieties contain. Its name is reminiscent of ratatouilles we've enjoyed in the south of France. It's a great way to get extra veggies in and is such a quick and easy way to enjoy homemade pizza, without having to make a base. Make sure you select firm, ripe eggplants with a smooth shiny skin.

SERVES   PREP TIME   COOK TIME

2 **eggplants** (aubergines)

2 Tbsp **olive oil**

Salt and **pepper**

1 cup **super seven sauce** (**pg 188**) or **tomato paste**

Toppings such as **olives**, **mushrooms**, **red onion**

150g (5oz) **grated cheese**

Variations:

Add diced fresh chilli for a spicier version.

Add pre-cooked strips of quality bacon, beef, lamb or chicken for omnivorous folk.

Swap the super seven sauce for harissa (**pg 194**), basil pesto (**pg 192**).

Children may prefer smaller circular mini-pizzas which you can create by cutting the eggplant crossways, rather than lengthways.

1. Preheat oven to 180°C (360°F). Cut each eggplant lengthways into four or five slices each approximately 1½ cm (½ inch) thick.

2. Oil two baking trays and dab the eggplant slices on both sides to coat with oil. Season with salt and pepper and roast for 6 minutes on one side.

3. Meanwhile make your super seven sauce if you don't have any on hand (**pg 188**). Prepare your toppings and grate the cheese.

4. Remove the eggplants from the oven. Turn them over on the tray and spread sauce on the newly upturned side, then add your toppings and cheese. Bake for about 6 minutes until the cheese is melted and starting to brown. Enjoy while hot.

Moroccan Lamb and Mint Meatballs

The spices and the mint in these meatballs really compliment the lamb. They are super simple to do being oven-baked rather than pan fried, and you can even opt for the meatloaf version if you want to save more time. Lamb is an excellent source of protein, iron and zinc which are all important for optimal health. Extra meatballs are a great addition to lunchboxes for young and old alike.

SERVES   PREP TIME   COOK TIME

500g (1lb) **lamb mince**

1 **onion**, finely diced

1 **carrot**, finely grated

1 cup fresh **mint leaves**, chopped

1 cup **rolled oats**

2 **eggs**

1 Tbsp **ground cumin**

1 Tbsp **ground coriander**

1 400g (14oz) can **diced tomatoes**

Salt and **pepper**

Variations:

To save time, you could skip forming the meatballs and simply make a meatloaf by pressing the mixture into a lined loaf tin and bake for 30 minutes. Omit the diced tomatoes in this case.

To liven things up add diced fresh chilli or chilli powder.

*For a gluten free option replace the rolled oats with gluten free breadcrumbs.

1. Preheat oven to 190°C (375°F). Dice the onion, grate the carrot and chop the mint. Combine these together in a large bowl with the lamb, oats, eggs, cumin, coriander, a pinch of salt and a grind of pepper.

2. With a soup spoon, scoop out golf ball size amounts and form them into balls with damp hands and place into a casserole dish.

3. Cook for 15 minutes, then turn the meatballs over and add the can of diced tomatoes with another pinch of salt and grind of pepper to form a sauce over and around them.

4. Return it to the oven and cook for a further 15 minutes. Serve hot with quinoa, brown rice or couscous and steamed greens.

4C Creamy Coconut Chicken Casserole

This is one of my favourite casseroles. I invented it on a whim one weekend when I had left over super seven sauce and chicken thighs on hand to cook. It turned out so well that we have repeated it often. It's the most highly viewed recipe on my website and I've had rave reviews from everyone that's tried it. Ask your butcher for deboned skinless chicken thighs. Thigh meat has more flavour than chicken breast, is less prone to drying out and is often less expensive as well.

SERVES 4   PREP TIME 10   COOK TIME 60   GF DF

- 4 free range **chicken thighs**, deboned, skin off
- 2 small **onions**
- 4 **potatoes**
- 2 **carrots**
- 1-2 cups **super seven sauce (pg 188) harissa (pg 194)** or **tomato paste**
- 1 400ml (14fl oz) can **coconut cream**
- **Salt** and **pepper**

1. Preheat the oven to 180°C (360°F). Heat a fry pan on high. Brown the chicken thighs with a little oil for 2-3 minutes on each side.

2. Meanwhile peel and halve the onions and clean the potatoes and carrots (leaving the skin on) and chop them into similar sized pieces. Place these into a roasting dish then transfer the pieces of chicken, placing them on top of the vegetables.

3. Coat the chicken pieces in the super seven sauce, harissa or tomato paste depending on what you have on hand. Pour over the can of coconut cream and season well.

4. Cook for 45 minutes to 1 hour, basting the chicken and vegetables from time to time. Allow some of the tomato sauce to mix through with the coconut cream while also allowing some to thicken and stick to the chicken in all its deliciousness!

5. Serve hot with lightly steamed greens on the side.

166 dinners

Note – This meal freezes well so I usually make a double batch in two separate dishes and freeze one as an instant family meal for another night.

Easy Kumara and Lentil Dahl

This is a lovely warming dahl with lots of flavour from the aromatic spices. It is packed with fibre, protein and antioxidants from the vegetables and the spices also have wonderful anti-inflammatory properties. Leftovers freeze well so I always make at least a double batch of this recipe.

SERVES PREP TIME COOK TIME

- 1 Tbsp oil
- 1 Tbsp each of ground cumin, coriander and turmeric
- 2 Tbsp curry powder
- 4 cloves garlic, crushed
- 2 400g (14oz) cans diced tomatoes
- 2 cups liquid stock
- 500g (1lb) kumara (sweet potato)
- 500g (1lb) dry red lentils
- 250g spinach, fresh or frozen
- Salt and pepper

Variations:

Add a diced fresh chilli or chilli powder for a spicier version.

*For a vegetarian option, ensure that you use vegetable stock.

*Omit yoghurt or labneh for a dairy free version.

1. Heat a large high sided fry pan or pot with oil. Add the spices and garlic and cook for 2-3 minutes until aromatic. Meanwhile peel and cut the kumara into 1 inch chunks.

2. Add the diced tomatoes, stock, kumara and lentils. Season with salt and pepper and simmer for 15 minutes.

3. Blend with a stick blender in the pot, or for a more textured dahl you can choose to leave it as is.

4. Lastly, add the spinach. Taste and season with salt and pepper as desired. Simmer for a further 5 minutes.

5. Serve hot with rice or quinoa and a dollop of natural yoghurt or labneh.

Succulent Lemon Roast Chicken

There is something special about sharing a roast meal such as this with family and friends. It smells delicious, looks amazing on the table and creates a great anticipation. The lemon is the secret weapon of this recipe which is sure to become a favourite in your home. I like to make this meal go further by setting aside leftover root vegetables for a salad or frittata the next day, saving leftover chicken for salads or wraps, and I then use the remaining carcass to make chicken stock.

SERVES   PREP TIME   COOK TIME

1 medium free range chicken

10 cups (1kg, 2lbs) roasting vegetables – potatoes, carrots, pumpkin (squash), kumara (sweet potato)

1 onion, quartered

6 garlic cloves, skin on

2-3 Tbsp olive oil

3 lemons, juiced and zested

Salt and pepper

1. Preheat oven to 180°C (360°F) with a baking dish inside. Leaving the skins on, cut the root vegetables into similar sizes.

2. Par boil the vegetables in salted water for 8-12 minutes until just undercooked. You may want to separate the different types to ensure they all cook to a similar tenderness. Drain them and give them a good shake in the pot allowing the steam to rise. This allows them to go slightly crumbly around the edges, which will create lovely crispy deliciousness once roasted.

3. Carefully oil your now hot baking dish. Add the par boiled vegetables along with the quartered onion and garlic cloves and give them a shake around to coat.

4. Place the chicken on top. Season with salt and pepper. Finely zest and juice the lemon into a small bowl and pour this over chicken and vegetables.

5. Oven bake for around 1 ½ hours spooning the juices back over it all 2-3 times during cooking. If you prefer crispier vegetables, half way through the cook time, move them into a separate pan or baking tray and spread them out well, turning them every 20 minutes.

6. Slice into the chicken to check that it is well cooked and the juices run clear. Carve and serve hot with the roasted vegetables and lightly steamed greens.

French Lamb and Date Tajine

My French host-dad Jean-Michel taught my husband and I this recipe which uses his favourite spice blend. It may look like a long list of ingredients, but I can assure you it is worth it! The spices are beautifully aromatic and have anti-inflammatory and antioxidant properties. Lamb is an excellent source of protein, iron and zinc and the mixture of vegetables offer a wide range of nutrients and fibre. This is an easy meal to slow cook all day, or if you have one, cook it in a tajine dish to impress your guests when you place it on the table!

SERVES 4-6 PREP TIME 10 COOK TIME 2+ HRS   GF DF

1.2kg (2½ lbs) **lamb on the bone** (knuckles or chops work well)

1 400g (14oz) **kumara** (sweet potato)

2 **carrots**

1 handful **green beans**

6 **garlic cloves**, in their skins

½ cup (60g, 2oz) **dates**

1 400g (14oz) can of **diced tomatoes**

2 Tbsp **balsamic vinegar**

Tajine spice mix

2 tsp **sweet paprika**

2 tsp **ground coriander**

1 tsp **ground cumin**

1 tsp **garam masala**

1 tsp **curry powder**

½ tsp **turmeric**

Pinch **chilli powder**

Salt and **pepper**

1. Heat the oven to 160°C (320°F). Mix the spices together in a small bowl.

2. Peel the kumara and cut it and the carrots into similar size chunks. Trim the ends off the beans.

3. Combine everything in a tajine or casserole dish with a lid and cook for 2-3 hours. Alternatively this meal can be cooked all day in a slow cooker.

4. Serve hot with fresh bread or wholemeal couscous to soak up the delicious sauce. Bon appetit!

Note – This delicious spice blend is well worth making up in bulk to use regularly. To do so, use a 1/8 cup measure in place of a tsp to multiply the quantities. Mix it together and store your spice mix in an airtight jar, using 2 tablespoons for this recipe.

Simple Baked Salmon

Salmon is packed full of essential omega-3 oils which the majority of people are lacking from their diet. Every time I make this dish it reminds me of my French host-mum Béatrice who first taught me how to bake salmon. It is incredibly easy to do (read fail proof!) and brings out the simple flavour of the salmon accentuated by the citrus.

SERVES PREP TIME COOK TIME

½ cup **quinoa**

½ head of **broccoli**, cut in florets

2 Tbsp **olive oil**

4 x 200g (7oz) **salmon fillets**

2 **lemons**

2 **tomatoes**, quartered

Salt and **pepper**

1. Pre heat oven to 180°C (360°F). Start the quinoa cooking and place the broccoli in a bowl covered with boiling water for five minutes.

2. Add oil to a baking dish, add the salmon fillets turning them to coat them in oil, leaving them skin side down.

3. Slice 1 lemon placing slices on top of the salmon. Add the tomatoes and broccoli, squeeze the second lemon's juice over everything and season it all with salt and pepper.

4. Bake for 15 minutes, or until little white beads start to pop out the sides of the salmon. Fluff the quinoa up with a fork and serve it all while hot.

Note – Choose salmon fillets that are all the same size to ensure even cooking.

Naturally Good Chocolate Brownie

Chocolate lovers will adore this rich brownie which is packed with goodness. With all natural ingredients giving precious antioxidants, it is the perfect healthy alternative to your typical sugar laden brownie. This pairs perfectly with the unbelievably good ice cream over the page. Enjoy!

SERVES PREP TIME COOK TIME

⅓ cup **cacao** or **cocoa powder**

1 cup **wholemeal flour**

1 tsp **baking soda**

¼ tsp **salt**

90g (3oz) **dark chocolate**, chopped

60g (2oz) **raw walnuts**, chopped

1 cup **stewed apple***

¾ cup **date puree***

*See the recipes for these natural sweeteners on **pg 200**.

Variations:

Substitute the walnuts for any other nuts. Almonds, pecans and pistachios all work well.

Top with frozen raspberries just pressed into mixture before cooking.

Cook in mini muffin tins for 15-20 minutes to make individual round brownies.

1. Preheat the oven to 170°C (340°F) and line a square baking dish.

2. Combine the first four dry ingredients in a bowl.

3. Chop the chocolate and nuts and mix in all the remaining ingredients until just combined. Avoid over-mixing.

4. Transfer to the baking dish and press down flat. Cook for 25-30 minutes until set in the centre. Allow to cool for 10 minutes before cutting with a sharp knife.

176 *desserts*

Unbelievably Good Ice Cream

Nothing could be more simple or refreshing than this great all natural dessert. You can serve it plain, or jazz it up with extra flavours and toppings – you decide! I always keep some bananas on hand in the freezer. It is best to remove the skin and chop them into quarters, then freeze them for ease of use later on. There is this wonderful moment as this recipe blends, where the bananas turn from chunks into this beautiful pale-yellow, smooth whipped ice cream. You really have to see it to believe it!

SERVES PREP TIME

4 ripe **bananas**, frozen in chunks

1 Tbsp **honey** or **pure maple syrup** (optional)

Extra flavours

Chocolate – 2 Tbsp cacao or cocoa powder

Vanilla – 2 tsp pure vanilla extract

Canadian – 1 Tbsp maple syrup and chopped walnuts

Berry – ½ cup frozen berries

Tropical – pulp of one passionfruit and ½ cup pineapple pieces or feijoa flesh

Nutty – ½ cup raw almonds, cashews or pistachios

1. In a food processor with an S blade, pulse and then blend the frozen banana chunks until they form a smooth creamy texture. Add the sweetener if using it.

2. Enjoy as is, or add extra flavours as desired. To make a mixture of different flavours, simply remove some of the ice cream and mix in each flavour in separate bowls. For the berry, tropical and nutty versions, add the extra flavours to the processor and blend them together.

3. Either serve immediately as a soft serve ice cream, or scrape the mixture into a container and re-freeze it for 4 or more hours, then serve with an ice cream scoop.

Perfect Pumpkin Pie

This is pumpkin pie with a twist; no pastry. Even better this super easy recipe requires no chopping! Simply buy a pre-cut segment of pumpkin which you can roast as is. Pumpkin is a great low GI, slow release energy source. It is packed with fibre, minerals, and phytochemicals that support optimal health, plus the cinnamon in this recipe helps stabilise blood sugar levels and is both anti-inflammatory and an antioxidant, so it really packs a punch for your health.

SERVES PREP TIME COOK TIME

- 3 cups **roasted pumpkin** (squash)
- 1 cup **dates**
- ½ cup **boiling water**
- ⅔ cup **milk**
- 2 Tbsp **oil**
- 2 tsp **vanilla extract**
- ¾ cup **wholemeal flour**
- 1 tsp **baking powder**
- 2 tsp **cinnamon**
- 1 tsp **ground ginger**
- 1 tsp **nutmeg**
- Pinch of **salt**

Variation:

*For a gluten free version you can replace the flour with 1 cup almond meal and reduce the milk to ¼ cup.

1. You can save time by using leftover roast pumpkin from another meal. Otherwise, leaving the skin on, place your pumpkin pieces in a covered oven dish with a dash of water. Roast at 180°C (360°F) for 40 minutes until soft. Once cooled, remove any seeds and scoop out 3 cups of flesh.

2. Add the dates and water to your food processor and leave them to soak for a few minutes while you grease or line a round spring-form cake tin.

3. Set the oven to 160°C (320°F). Blend the dates until smooth. Then add the pumpkin flesh, milk, oil, and vanilla and blend well.

4. Add the dry ingredients and blend until just combined, pour the mixture into your prepared pie dish and bake for 40 minutes.

5. Allow it to cool then transfer to the fridge to set for 2-3 hours before slicing. Serve with Greek yoghurt or labneh.

Secret Chocolate Mousse

This mousse is dairy and egg free and keeps for up to a week in your fridge (if it lasts that long!) It is great for entertaining as you can make it in advance, layer it in tall glasses and greatly impress your guests. Avocado is packed with healthy fats, honey is a great natural sweetener with anti-bacterial properties and cacao is rich in antioxidants. If you have any non-avocado fans you might just avoid telling them what's in it and see if they can figure it out. This recipe has fooled many a dinner party guest of my clients over the years. Enjoy trying it out yourself!

SERVES 4   PREP TIME 10   GF   DF   V

It is so simple, just three ingredients…

3 large ripe **avocados**

⅓ cup **honey**

⅓ cup **cacao** or **cocoa powder**

1. Quarter the avocados lengthways and remove the stones. Peel the skins off and place the flesh in a food processor.

2. Add the other ingredients and blend until smooth. Check that there are no lumps, scrape down the sides and re-blend just to be sure! Taste test and adjust the flavors by adding more honey, cacao or cocoa as desired.

3. Serve in tall glasses layered together with labneh or natural yoghurt and fruit such as banana, kiwifruit, blueberries, raspberries or strawberries.

 Go to www.bit.ly/CWLChocolateMousse for a step by step demonstration video.

Note - This recipe is wonderful as a chocolate ganache for cakes, as a dipping sauce or anywhere else you love chocolate.

Banoffee Pie

This is a completely natural version of what is traditionally a very rich and unhealthy dessert. The cashews and yoghurt offer protein and healthy fats, while the dates and banana bring a natural sweetness and fibre. It is easy to slice and serve and is sure to impress your friends and family! Best of all this is super simple to make (you can even pre-make and freeze the base and centre, so I usually make two at a time and freeze one for a later date).

SERVES 12 PREP TIME 15 COOK TIME 8 GF DF* V

Base

3 Tbsp coconut oil, melted
1 cup rolled oats
½ cup desiccated coconut
½ cup raw cashews
8 dried dates

Centre

1 cup raw cashews
1 ½ cups dried dates
1 tsp vanilla extract
1 large banana

Topping

2 bananas, sliced
¾ cup Greek yoghurt

1. Preheat the oven to 160°C (320°F). Place the base ingredients in a food processor with an S blade and combine to form a crumb. Press down into a lined spring form tin or pie dish.

2. Bake for 6-8 minutes until light golden brown then allow to cool.

3. Meanwhile blend the centre measure of cashews for 2-3 minutes, pausing and scraping down as needed to form a paste. Then blend in the dates and vanilla. Lastly add the banana and blend until smooth. It is quite a sticky mixture so give your blender a break if it is heating up.

4. Once the base has cooled, pour the filling in and spread it out. It can be very sticky so use a metal spoon that has rested in a cup of boiling water to spread it evenly. Keep chilled until ready to serve.

5. Top with a layer of thinly sliced banana (saving some for a garnish) then a layer of Greek yoghurt spread out to the edge of the outside ring of banana slices. Garnish the centre with a few remaining pieces of banana.

Go to www.bit.ly/CWLBanoffee for a step by step demonstration video.

Variations:

*For a dairy free option, use coconut oil in the base and replace the yoghurt with the scooped out top half of a can of coconut cream which has been chilled in the fridge.

A delicious option is to serve this hot topped with unbelievably good ice cream (pg 178). Simply return the pie to the oven once you add the centre and cook for a further 8 minutes then serve it hot, topped with the cold banana ice cream. Enjoy!

Lemon Lime Pistachio Cheesecakes

This is such a simple unbaked and unconventional yet delicious cheesecake. The recipe is ridiculously easy to make and is guaranteed to impress friends at your next dinner party, or just for you and your special someone for your next date night. Serve them in your fanciest glasses and savour them slowly!

SERVES PREP TIME COOK TIME

Base

¾ cup **LSA** (ground linseed, sunflower and almond)

⅓ cup **natural pistachios,** chopped (save some as a garnish)

2 Tbsp **butter** or **coconut oil**, melted

Topping

200g (7oz) **ricotta**

1 cup Greek **yoghurt**

4 Tbsp **pure maple syrup**

1 **lime**, zest and juice (approx 2 Tbsp)

2 **lemons**, zest and juice (approx 6 Tbsp)

1. Mix the base ingredients in a bowl until combined. Spoon equal amounts into each glass. Press it down firmly and set aside in the fridge.

2. In a bowl, beat the ricotta and yoghurt together with a whisk or electric beaters.

3. Finely zest or peel and dice the lemons and lime (saving a little zest as a garnish). Juice them into a small bowl.

4. Add the maple syrup, most of the zest and half of the juice to the ricotta mixture and mix well. Taste and adjust the flavours, adding more juice or maple syrup as desired.

5. Spoon the topping into each glass and garnish with a few pistachios and the reserved lemon and lime zest.

6. Store in the fridge, or for firmer cheesecakes you can chill them in the freezer for 20 minutes prior to serving.

Note - You can prepare this dessert ahead of time and freeze them for up to 3 months. Give them 1-2 hours to semi-thaw at room temperature before serving.

Super Seven Sauce

This recipe combines the goodness of seven vegetables into a delicious sauce that will be loved by children and adults alike. Perfect for pizzas or as a pasta sauce, you can make up a fresh batch to serve with dinner and freeze extra portions for a quick and easy meal at a later date.

MAKES PREP TIME COOK TIME

- 1 large **onion**, diced
- 2-3 **garlic cloves**, crushed
- 1 **carrot**, grated
- 1 **courgette** (zucchini), grated
- 1 **capsicum** (bell pepper), diced
- 2 400g (14oz) cans **diced tomatoes**
- 4 Tbsp **tomato paste**
- 1 bunch **parsley**

Variations:

Add quality ham or bacon.

Add roasted root vegetables or eggplant (aubergines) to make a thicker sauce.

1. In a pan brown the onion and garlic with a little oil.

2. Add the remaining ingredients and let it simmer gently for 10-12 minutes allowing the sauce to reduce.

3. Remove from the heat and blend with a stick blender until smooth.

Bright Beet Hummus

Quick and simple, bright and beautiful! This recipe is my go-to if I have unexpected guests or an impromptu social gathering to attend and want a delicious platter of nibbles at short notice. Packed with antioxidants and fibre this condiment is great as a dip but also works well in wraps, dolloped on salads or pizzas, or as a garnish with your main.

SERVES   PREP TIME

1 400g (14oz) can **chickpeas** (garbanzo beans)

1 400g (14oz) can **sliced beetroot** (beets)

1-2 cloves **garlic**

1 Tbsp **olive oil**

Salt and **pepper**

1. Drain the beetroot and reserve the juice. Drain and rinse the chickpeas.

2. Shell and roughly chop the garlic. Blend everything together in a food processor adding beetroot juice as required to reach your desired consistency.

3. Chill and serve with sliced veges, wholegrain crackers, pitas cut in to triangles or even with homemade hot chips or wedges.

4. Store in the fridge and use within 1 week. If you have more than enough you can freeze any excess into ice cube trays, then pop them out once frozen and store in a zip lock bag ready for ease of use later on.

 Go to www.bit.ly/CWLBeetHummus for a step by step demonstration video.

Parsley and Basil Pesto

This pesto adds a huge amount of flavour and is the perfect accompaniment to almost any meal. Spread it on pizza, dollop it onto salads, mix it through as a pasta sauce, add it to burgers or wraps, coat chicken, salmon, beef or lamb with it and bake, or simply serve it along with a platter of vegetable sticks. Packed full of antioxidants and healthy fats this makes a wonderful nutritious condiment, free of preservatives and additives.

MAKES   PREP TIME

- 3 Tbsp cashews or pine nuts
- 2 cups basil leaves
- 1 cup parsley
- 1 shallot
- 2 cloves garlic
- 1 Tbsp lemon juice
- 4 Tbsp extra virgin olive oil
- salt and pepper

1. Dry toast the nuts in a hot pan for 2-3 minutes until golden.

2. Combine all ingredients less the olive oil and seasoning in a blender and process well. Pause and scrape down the sides as needed to ensure everything is well combined.

3. Stream in the olive oil while blending then season it to taste.

4. Store in a glass jar in the fridge and use within one month. If you have more than enough, you can freeze any excess into ice cube trays, then pop them out once frozen and store in a zip lock bag ready for ease of use later on.

Harissa

Harissa comes from North Africa and is fantastic spread on wraps and pizzas, as a crust on roast lamb, beef or chicken, or it can be used as a dip in an antipasto platter. For ease, this recipe uses tomato paste; alternatively you can use diced tomatoes and allow it to simmer for an extra hour or so to reduce the sauce. Either way, the end result is a lovely smooth, thick tomato sauce with a great depth of flavour from the spices, vinegar and garlic. Caution – Once you have tasted this sauce you may become addicted!

MAKES 2 Jars   PREP TIME 15   GF DF V

- 4 Tbsp ground coriander
- 3 Tbsp ground cumin
- 3 Tbsp sweet paprika
- 1 500g (1lb) jar of tomato paste
- 8 garlic cloves, crushed
- 2 Tbsp balsamic or red wine vinegar
- Salt and pepper
- ½ cup of olive oil

1. In a hot pan cook the spices with about 2 Tbsp of oil until fragrant.
2. Reduce the heat to medium. Crush and add the garlic, then the remaining ingredients and cook it through for a few minutes.
3. Taste and adjust the seasoning, adding extra spices as desired to create the taste you like.
4. Allow it to cool and pour into a clean glass jar. Store in the fridge and use within 3-4 weeks. If you make a big batch to store for longer, use sterilised jars and top with a layer of oil to prevent it oxidising.

Variations:

If you have the time, for the best flavour I highly recommend toasting and grinding your own spices to make this recipe. Dry toast whole coriander and cumin seeds in a hot pan for a few minutes until fragrant, then grind (in a spice grinder or with a mortar and pestle). The smell will be amazing and it really adds to the taste.

To give it a kick add either fresh or dried chillies, ground chilli powder or hot paprika. Cook them through from the start to take the raw edge off and add a little honey or date puree to balance the heat.

Labneh

Labneh is a Middle Eastern soft cheese made from yoghurt which is much like a cream cheese. It can be used in both sweet and savoury dishes, similar to a thicker version of Greek yoghurt. Stir it into soups or curries, dollop it onto salads, spread it onto toast or crackers, mix fresh herbs or spices through it and serve as a dip, or have it with fresh fruit, cinnamon and syrup as a delicious dessert.

MAKES   PREP TIME   WAIT TIME

500g (1lb) **full fat organic yoghurt**

½ tsp **salt**

1 square of **muslin** or **cheesecloth**

1. Place the cloth inside a sieve sitting in a large bowl. Salt the yoghurt and scoop it onto the cloth, tying the ends together in a knot. If you don't have a sieve, you can tie the knot around a large spoon or chopsticks and suspend it above a deep bowl.

2. Leave it in the fridge to strain off the liquid whey. After 8-12 hours it will have reached a smooth spreadable consistency. Leave it for up to 48 hours if you prefer a thicker version similar to regular cream cheese.

3. Store in the fridge and use within a week.

Labneh

Nut Butter

Nut butter can be made from a range of different nuts, such as peanuts, almonds, macadamia or hazelnuts. They all contain healthy fats which aid the absorption of certain vitamins, and which help curb cravings after a meal. Nut butter is a great snack spread on celery sticks, or apple slices, served with wholesome crackers or breads, used in baking, or mixed into satay style sauces.

MAKES   PREP TIME   COOK TIME

750g (1½lb) **peanuts** or other **nuts**
½ tsp **salt**
Olive oil

Variations:

For a crunchy version pause the blender when the nuts are coarsely broken up and remove about a cup of nut pieces. Continue as normal then add these in right at the end, then blend again very briefly.

You can also make up a blend using a mixture of different nuts as desired.

1. Heat the oven to 160°C (320°F). Roast nuts in a large roasting pan for about 10-15 minutes stirring every 3-4 minutes until the centres are golden brown and they have a great flavour. Take care not to burn them.

2. Remove and transfer them to a cold tray to help them cool quickly.

3. Once cooled, blend the roasted nuts in a food processor with an S blade along with the salt until finely blended.

4. With the blades turning, drizzle in oil one spoonful at a time to reach your desired consistency. The amount of oil you will need will depend greatly on how oily the nuts are.

5. Store in a glass jar in the fridge and use within 2 months. The oil will rise to the top so you may want to mix it a little before use.

Natural Sweeteners

These sweeteners are great alternatives to refined sugar for use in baking, casseroles, curries and sauces. They provide sweetness as well as natural fibre and nutrients. You can store them in an airtight jar in the fridge and use them over 2-3 weeks, or freeze them into ice cube trays or muffin tins and defrost them as needed.

Date Puree

MAKES   PREP TIME

2 cups **dates**

1 cup **boiling water**

1. Place dates and boiling water in food processor with an S blade. Leave them to soak for 5 minutes then blend until smooth.

Stewed Apple

MAKES   PREP TIME   COOK TIME

3-4 **apples**

½ cup **hot water**

1. Cut apples into slices removing the cores, leaving the skin on.

2. Place them in a pot with the water and bring to a gentle simmer with the lid on.

3. Cook stirring occasionally for 15 minutes until soft then blend with a stick blender in the pot.

Immunity Boosting Smoothie

This is an incredibly refreshing drink, which boosts your immune system to keep you feeling great. The ginger gives it a lovely zingy taste and works as a powerful antioxidant and anti-inflammatory. The citrus fruits and vegetables add vitamins, fibre and goodness, while the honey has anti-bacterial properties making this a well-rounded drink to help you stave off, or recover more quickly from an illness. You can adjust the amount of ginger and honey to suit your taste.

SERVES 2   PREP TIME 5   GF   DF   V

- 2 oranges, peeled
- 1 lemon, peeled
- 1 carrot, chunked
- 1 celery stick, chunked
- 1-2 tsp fresh ginger root, diced
- 1-2 tsp honey
- ½ - 1 cups ice

1. Place everything in a blender in the order shown and blend until smooth.
2. Add extra water to reach the consistency you desire.

Variations:

Add spinach or baby kale leaves for a light green smoothie.

Add raw garlic, if you can tolerate the taste, for extra health boosting benefits.

Note - This recipe will keep up to 48 hours in the fridge so you can save time by making one smoothie to last two days.

Green Vitality Smoothie

This is a fantastic way to get fresh raw greens into your day. Leafy greens are an excellent source of nutrients and protective antioxidants such as vitamins A, C, iron and folate. The banana and avocado give this smoothie a thick creamy texture that makes it really satisfying. Think of this as part of your health insurance policy, by including one of these daily before you head to work, or as a mid-morning or post-exercise snack. The chocolate version is especially good for getting children, or other non-green-lovers, hooked on the goodness of smoothies.

SERVES PREP TIME

1 **kiwifruit**

1 large **banana**, fresh or frozen

2 cups fresh **spinach leaves**

1 small **avocado**

½ cup **ice**

Variations:

Add 2 Tbsp cacao or cocoa powder and substitute the water for milk for a chocolate version.

Add pineapple or mango and substitute the water for coconut water for a tropical version.

Add 1 Tbsp of chia seeds or linseeds for extra healthy fats and protein.

1. Add all ingredients to the blender in the order shown.

2. Start blending by pulsing, then blend continuously until the spinach is well blended through.

3. Add approximately 1 cup of water or the amount you prefer to reach your desired consistency.

Note - This recipe will keep up to 48 hours in the fridge so you can save time by making one smoothie to last two days.

Hot Lemon and Ginger

This is a wonderful warming drink that supports your immune system. The ginger is both anti-inflammatory and an antioxidant, the lemon brings loads of vitamin C and the honey provides a lovely flavour balance, as well as soothing the throat and having anti-bacterial properties.

SERVES PREP TIME

½ inch of fresh ginger root, thinly sliced

1 lemon, sliced

1 Tbsp honey

Boiling water

1. Leaving the skin on, slice the ginger and lemon, removing any loose pips.

2. Place into a mug along with the honey and pour the boiling water over and leave it to steep for 2-3 minutes.

3. Allow it to cool slightly or add a dash of cold water before drinking.

Authentic Spiced Chai Latte

I had the pleasure of being taught this recipe in person by my Indian friend Manisha after an amazing home cooked lunch we shared with her and her family. She has a well-earnt reputation as one of the best chai makers in her neighbourhood. She sees chai as a cure-all, adding extra cloves in winter, and using it as a preventive measure if anyone in the family starts coming down with an illness. This drink will warm you, assist digestion and boost immunity. It is a firm favourite in our home. We tend to make a big batch and keep some in the fridge to enjoy over the next two days.

SERVES PREP TIME

- 4 **cinnamon sticks**
- 4 **cardamom pods**
- 4 **cloves**
- 2 tsp **fennel seeds**
- 4 **black tea bags** (or 2 Tbsp loose leaf tea)
- 1 Tbsp **honey** (optional)
- 6 cups **boiling water**
- 2 cups **milk**
- 1-2 inches of fresh **ginger root**, sliced

Variations:

*You can serve this tea black if you prefer, making it a dairy free option.

Use decaffeinated tea for a child friendly decaf version.

You can make chai tea ice blocks by freezing the cooled mixture in ice block moulds.

1. Put all ingredients less the milk into a pot and bring to the boil.
2. Simmer at a steady boil for 5 minutes to allow all of the flavours to be drawn out of the tea leaves, herbs and spices.
3. Add the milk then bring it back up to temperature.
4. Drain it through a fine sieve to remove the spices and serve hot.

Beautiful Banana Biscuits

My husband reckons that these are the best biscuits I've ever made. After 13 years of marriage I guess that's saying a lot! Soft centred and crunchy on the outside they are a delicious energy boosting snack. Naturally sweetened and free of refined flour, your skin and brain will love the healthy fats, minerals and vitamins included. You will also enjoy filling your home with the incredible aroma of these biscuits as they bake!

MAKES 　PREP TIME 　COOK TIME 　　

- 1 cup raw cashews (pre-soaked)
- ½ cup sultanas
- 2 cups desiccated coconut
- 2 cups sunflower and/or pumpkin seeds (pepitas)
- ½ tsp cinnamon (optional)
- 2 bananas
- 4 Tbsp coconut oil, warmed
- 3 Tbsp pure maple syrup
- 1 tsp vanilla extract

1. Preheat the oven to 165°C (330°F) and prepare two oven trays with baking paper.

2. Soak the cashews ideally for 2-3 hours covered in warm water on the bench with a pinch of salt. If you are short on time just soak the cashews for a few minutes while you assemble the other ingredients. Rinse and drain the cashews, then blend in a food processor with an S blade for 3 minutes.

3. In the meantime in a large bowl, mix together the sultanas, coconut, seeds and cinnamon.

4. Add the banana, coconut oil, maple syrup and vanilla to the food processor and blend until it is all well combined, scraping down the sides as needed.

5. Scrape the banana mixture into the bowl with the dry ingredients and mix well. It should be a moist sticky mixture that results. Add water if too dry or extra coconut if too moist.

6. Spoon the mixture out to form biscuit shapes. Bake for 15-20 minutes until golden brown. Then remove and transfer to a cooling rack. Take care as they will be quite soft while hot and will firm up as they cool.

7. These store well in an airtight container in the pantry for 1-2 days or fridge for 2-3 days. Freeze any extras that you won't use in that timeframe, or give them as gifts!

Choc Nut Bliss Slice

Reminiscent of the most decadent chocolate and nut bars, these offer you a nutritious alternative that will delight your taste buds. The oils and proteins in these nuts are fantastic for your brain, skin, hair and nails. The fruit adds a natural sweetness and the fibre makes these a satisfying mid-afternoon pick me up snack.

SERVES PREP TIME CHILL TIME

1 cup raw walnuts (pre-soaked)
1 cup raw almonds (pre-soaked)
1 cup rolled oats
1½ cups sultanas
3 Tbsp nut butter (see pg 198, or a quality store bought variety)
3 Tbsp cacao or cocoa powder

Icing

80g (3oz) dark chocolate
1 Tbsp coconut oil
A few walnuts to decorate

1. Soak the walnuts and almonds ideally for 6-12 hours covered in water with a pinch of salt. If you are short on time however, just soak them for a few minutes while you assemble the other ingredients.

2. Rinse and drain the water off then blend the nuts for 2-3 minutes in a food processor with an S blade.

3. Add all the remaining ingredients and blend well. You may need to add about 2-3 tablespoons of water if the mix is too dry. Blend it until it starts pulling away from the sides of the blender and forming a ball.

4. Press into a square slice tin lined with baking paper and chill while you melt the chocolate.

5. Melt the chocolate and coconut oil together (the oil makes it easier to slice later on once it's set) spread this evenly over the slice and top it with diced walnuts. Refrigerate for at least 20 minutes then cut.

6. Keep those you wish to use within 2-3 days in an airtight container in the fridge and freeze the rest. Keep chilled before serving.

Spinach, Feta and Mint Muffins

These tasty savoury muffins are lovely served warmed up and make great portable snacks for lunches or your next picnic. Spinach is a powerhouse of nutrition being an excellent source of vitamin A, C, iron and folate. Together with the mint and feta this is a delicious way to get more of it into your diet. These muffins freeze well so you can free flow them and pop them in a bag or lunchbox and they'll be ready to eat by mid-morning.

MAKES   PREP TIME   COOK TIME

2 eggs

1 cup milk

⅓ cup oil

150g (5oz) feta cheese, crumbled

250g (9oz) frozen spinach, thawed

1 cup mint, chopped

2 cups wholemeal flour

2 tsp baking powder

¼ tsp each salt and pepper

6 cherry tomatoes (optional)

¼ cup grated tasty or parmesan cheese

1. Preheat the oven to 180°C (360°F) and line or grease a muffin tray.

2. In a mixing bowl, beat together the eggs, milk and oil. Then add the feta, spinach and mint.

3. Add the flour, baking powder, salt and pepper and gently mix until just combined. Avoid over mixing.

4. Spoon the mixture into muffin trays and top with the halved cherry tomatoes and grated cheese.

5. Bake for 20 minutes, until light golden brown and a skewer comes out clean from the centre. Leave to cool for 5 minutes, then turn the muffins out onto a wire rack to cool.

Note – This is a great recipe to use up any leftover vegetables such as small broccoli florets, peas or corn. Add them in place of, or as well as, the spinach.

Citrus Squares

These scrumptious sweet treats are perfect for high tea with friends, through to school lunchboxes. Being raw, these really pack a punch with the fresh flavour from the lemons, along with their rich supply of vitamin C. The cashews and LSA add extra antioxidants, healthy fats, zinc and magnesium.

MAKES PREP TIME CHILL TIME

- 1 cup **raw cashews** (pre-soaked)
- 2 large **lemons**, zest and juice (about 4 Tbsp)
- 4 Tbsp **honey**
- 3 Tbsp **coconut oil**, melted
- 1 cup **LSA** (ground linseed, sunflower and almond)
- 1½ cups **desiccated coconut**
- A good pinch of **salt**

1. Soak the cashews ideally for 2-3 hours covered in warm water with a pinch of salt. If you are short on time just soak the cashews for a few minutes while you assemble the other ingredients. Rinse and drain, then blend in a food processor with an S blade for 3 minutes.

2. Meanwhile zest then juice lemons. Add all the ingredients and blend until combined, pausing and scraping the mixture down from the sides with a spatula as required.

3. The mixture will start pulling away from the sides as you blend. Add more desiccated coconut if the mixture is too moist or extra lemon juice or water if too dry. Taste test and add extra lemon or honey as needed.

4. Once the mixture is well blended, press it out into an oblong slice tin lined with baking paper. Chill for 20 minutes or more then cut into squares.

5. Keep those you wish to use within 2-3 days in an airtight container in the fridge and freeze the rest. Keep chilled before serving.

Variations:

You can roll the mixture into ping pong sized balls, then coat each ball in extra coconut.

Swap one of the lemons for two limes to add an extra zesty kick.

For a nut free version, replace the cashews with sunflower seeds and the LSA with rolled oats and add a little extra coconut oil.

Quinoa Quiche

My mum makes a fabulous zucchini slice which my whole family loves. This is a variation on that recipe with quinoa in place of the standard flour. Quinoa is a complete form of protein and together with the eggs this makes an excellent protein and fibre packed addition to your children's (or your own) lunchboxes. It also makes for a great breakfast, lunch or a light dinner.

MAKES PREP TIME COOK TIME

- 1 cup cooked quinoa
- 6 eggs
- 2 courgettes (zucchini), grated
- 1 carrot, grated
- 1 onion, finely diced
- 4 slices quality bacon, diced
- 1 cup tasty cheese, grated
- ¼ cup oil
- salt and pepper

Variations:

*Omit the bacon for a vegetarian option.

Bake the mixture in muffin or mini muffin trays to make mini quichelets. (My girls call these cheese crunchies and they are ever popular!)

1. It's easiest to use leftover pre-cooked quinoa from a previous meal, but if you don't have any on hand, begin by cooking ½ cup of raw quinoa.

2. Preheat the oven to 175°C (350°F) and grease or line an oblong slice tray.

3. Grate the vegetables and cheese and dice the onion and bacon.

4. Combine all ingredients in a large bowl and mix well. Pour the mixture out into the tray and bake for 25 minutes until golden.

5. Cut into slices or squares and serve hot or chilled. Keep what you will use within the next few days in the fridge and freeze the remainder.

Ginger Fudge Slice

This soft gooey fudge style version of a ginger slice is quite delectable. Made from all natural raw ingredients, the ginger adds incredible flavour, as well as being a fantastic antioxidant and anti-inflammatory. The healthy fats in the nuts and coconut oil make this a satisfying snack which is fitting for the fanciest high tea party or as a light dessert.

MAKES PREP TIME CHILL TIME

Base

½ cup **raw almonds** (pre-soaked)
½ cup **rolled oats**
10 dried **dates**
3 Tbsp **coconut oil**, melted

Topping

2 cups **raw cashews** (pre-soaked)
2 Tbsp fresh **ginger root**, diced
2 Tbsp **coconut oil**, melted
3 Tbsp **pure maple syrup**
1 tsp **vanilla extract**
A good pinch of **salt**

1. Soak the almonds and cashew nuts in separate bowls of water with a pinch of salt. Ideally soak the almonds for 6-12 hours and the cashew nuts for 2-3 hours. But if all else fails, just give them a few minutes while you assemble the other ingredients.

2. Rinse and drain the almonds, then blend all of the base ingredients together in a food processor with an S blade for about 3 minutes until well combined and forming a fine crumb.

3. Press this into a square slice tin lined with baking paper and chill in the fridge while you prepare the topping.

4. Blend the cashews and ginger root for 3-4 minutes scraping the sides down a couple of times until it forms a creamy paste.

5. Add all of the remaining ingredients and blend well.

6. Scrape the topping out and smooth it out carefully over the base with the back of a metal spoon. Return the slice to the fridge for 20 minutes to chill.

7. Slice and keep those you wish to use within 2-3 days in an airtight container in the fridge and freeze the rest. Keep chilled before serving.

– PART VIII –

Live Well Principles

I believe that a holistic approach is essential to total wellbeing, which is why I have developed five **Live Well Principles**. Each principle is underpinned by six pillars and I've seen how powerful they are to change lives when applied together. I know they will transform your life as you build them into your daily habits.

This book has explained **Nourish** in great depth, but hasn't addressed the other four principles – **Uplift**, **Invigorate**, **Strengthen**, or **Restore**. As I believe balance is essential in life I want to share the wider context that *real food less fuss* fits within.

This section of the book gives you an insight into my complete approach to total health and wellbeing. As often as possible I encourage you to find ways to incorporate several pillars in your daily life simultaneously.

For example you can enjoy outdoor restorative movement while connecting with others, which covers three pillars from the restore **Invigorate**, **Strengthen** and **Restore** principles at the same time. Or you can practise gratitude, breathing deeply while savouring a real food meal, covering the **Uplift**, **Restore** and **Nourish** principles simultaneously.

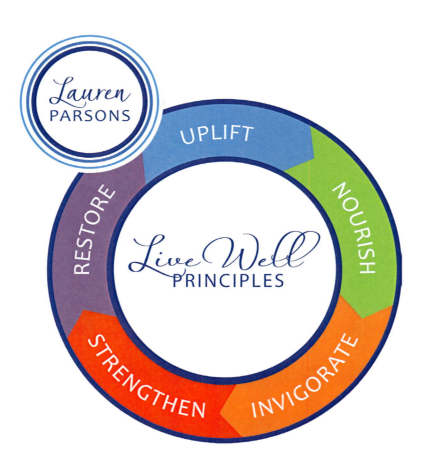

Uplift

Think Well
Positive Focus
Attitude of Gratitude
Positive Self-Talk
Constant Learning
Complete Communication

Nourish

Eat Real Food
Nutrient Dense
Positive Relationship with Food
Cook Fast, Eat Slow
Savour Food Mindfully
Hydrate

Invigorate

Active Attitude
Snack on Exercise
Add Intensity
Sit Less, Move More
Play
Time Outdoors

Strengthen

Strength Train
Quality vs Quantity
Stand Strong
Build Resilience
Strong Mind
Social Connection

Restore

Breathe
Stay in Rhythm
Sleep Well
Restorative Movement
Trust
Be Present

Uplift

Think Well

Our thoughts are incredibly powerful. They determine our words, our actions, our day to day habits and ultimately our lives. The great thing is that we have the power to direct our thoughts. Being aware of what we expose ourselves to, the words we take on board, our self-talk and where we choose to direct our thoughts influences how we behave day to day.

Our lives are a sum of our daily habits. As you learn to interrupt unhelpful thinking patterns and replace them with the truth you will be calmer, more relaxed and able to fully enjoy life.

Positive Goals

What we focus on increases in our lives, so it is incredibly important to focus on what we want. Often we do the opposite and spend time thinking about our problems, life's challenges and all of the things that we don't want to happen, which tends to get us stuck.

Setting goals and aspirations in the positive tense e.g. "I want to be vibrant and energised" rather than "I don't want to feel so tired and flat" will transform your life. Choose to direct your thoughts towards the positive outcome you want, be mindful of the word "don't" (which your subconscious brain doesn't hear) and switch your thoughts around to a positive statement.

Having a clear vision of where you want to be and how you want life to be is a powerful way of switching on your internal motivation.

It trains your internal GPS to take you where you want to go.

Attitude of Gratitude

Gratitude makes what we have enough. Rather than focusing on our lack, focusing on our abundance transforms how we feel. No matter what situation you are in there is always something to be thankful for.

Our brains cannot focus on two things at once, so during challenging times it is especially important to practise gratitude, as it instantly shifts your perspective and changes your mood.

Daily journaling, thanking others, sharing your highs and taking time to count your blessings are all great ways to adopt an attitude of gratitude. Gratitude leads to even more good things occurring in your life because you get more of what you focus on. This creates an ever-increasing spiral, leading to even more gratitude.

Positive Self-Talk

The person we spend the most time listening to is ourselves. Our self-talk is the internal dialogue we have running in our minds throughout the day. Often we can fall into unhelpful patterns of thinking using unkind words and making untrue statements like "I'll never be good at this", "Stupid me" or "No-one would want me."

Limiting core beliefs like these cause us to doubt ourselves and rob us of self-confidence and self-esteem.

Resetting your self-talk and replacing it with the truth is essential to move forward into freedom. If you have been listening to negative audio recordings playing over in your mind, it is time to hit eject and to re-record over them with true life-giving statements.

Open to Learning

Curiosity is a wondrous thing. It allows you to enjoy life to the full. Being open to learning guarantees you will be able to overcome any obstacle in life.

We often learn best through making mistakes so the process of learning can feel uncomfortable. (Just think of learning to ride a bike).

Yet learning creates opportunities for growth, a fundamental human need, so it is important to push through that discomfort at times.

It is marvellous to feel the progress that occurs as our eyes are opened to new ideas.

Each time you step outside of your comfort zone, you will discover that your comfort zone enlarges, giving you the space to do and experience more things in life.

Complete Communication

Positive relationships are fundamental to our happiness and communication is the key that determines whether they will flourish and thrive, or not.

Complete communication is where we thoughtfully and respectfully express how we feel and what we want, with the goal of creating a positive ending where everyone's needs are met. It is a two-way process that involves excellent listening skills and requires us to take personal responsibility for how we feel.

It ensures we look at situations from other people's point of view, considering and expressing the benefits for them so as to reach positive outcomes for all parties.

Invigorate

Active Attitude

Modern technology and labour saving devices have made it easy to go days or even weeks without moving our bodies as they are designed to move. We need to intentionally adopt an active attitude, looking for and taking every opportunity to move our bodies. This not only strengthens muscles, it also boosts our mood and keeps us in great overall health.

Set your default to *active*, for example: walking briskly, taking the stairs, or commuting by bike or foot whenever possible. Find enjoyable ways to move by taking up active hobbies and socialising in ways that get you moving and you'll be set with great default habits for life.

Snack on Exercise

Snack on exercise in short sharp bursts that easily fit into your day. Could you pledge to be active for at least four minutes a day for the rest of your life? It will boost your mood, make you stronger, fitter, smarter, healthier and happier. Fitting in one minute snacks several times throughout the day takes virtually no extra time and is incredibly easy to maintain.

Your body is the best workout tool you could ever hope for. As you discover fun ways to get your heart rate up and/or strengthen your muscles, you will benefit from the life-giving benefits of exercise without having to add it to your already full to-do list. (For more information see www.SnackOnExercise.com)

Add Intensity

Intensity is vital to increasing fitness. Doing steady gentle exercise has far fewer benefits than when you add in a few short intervals of enthusiasm. Even endurance athletes will incorporate higher intensity training as it greatly improves their capacity to go the distance.

Because intensity has an inverse relationship with time you will see better results by training smarter not harder. Just picture trying to sprint for 20 minutes as opposed to 20 seconds. You could put a lot more effort into a short sprint right? That effort creates positive physiological and hormonal responses in the body.

Overcome the "fat-burning zone myth" which recommends gentle exercise, and instead harness the power of intensity. Bear in mind that intensity is relative to your fitness level. For you this may be walking briskly, jogging up an incline or doing an all out sprint. By adding intensity not only will you reap more short term benefits, you'll also become more efficient at burning fat, keeping you healthier long-term.

Sit Less, Move More

Sitting down for long episodes has serious negative consequences for our health. Even if we exercise at other times, extended periods of sitting are associated with higher mortality (death) and morbidity (sickness) rates.

If you have a predominantly sedentary role, find ways to break up the sitting. Whether you have a standing desk option or not, there are lots of ways to add movement into your day. For every hour that you sit, get up and move for a few minutes. Link it to routine activities such as phone calls, checking emails, filing or getting a glass of water.

Have standing meetings and create a deskercise routine that you enjoy. Encourage others around you to join in, making frequent movement the new norm.

Play

We are all born with an instinct to play. Children are naturally good at playing but because of societal norming most adults are not.

Adding playful movement and laughter back into our lives is beneficial on many levels. It helps build social connection, reduces stress, strengthens positive brain pathways and creates opportunities to move in natural and fluid ways.

If we enjoy something we will naturally want to do more of it.

Find fun ways to move and schedule in time and opportunities to play, encouraging others to join you.

Good natured competition can be highly motivating at all ages. Be childlike with the children in your life. They will love it and it will greatly enhance your relationship.

Time Outdoors

There is no substitute for spending time in nature, having the sun on our skin and being surrounded by plants and wildlife. It restores the soul, declutters the mind and uplifts the spirit.

When was the last time you walked barefoot on the beach or lay in the grass looking at the sky? Think how that would make you feel if you did it today.

Spending regular time outdoors where you can touch, smell and observe your natural environment, reduces stress and systemic inflammation and helps you feel more centred. Getting sunlight into our eyes near midday also improves sleep and mood.

Strengthen

Strength Train

Strength training is literally your fountain of youth! It reverses virtually all of the major biological signs of ageing. As we age our muscles naturally atrophy, yet strength training reverses that, rebuilding lean muscle, boosting metabolism and strengthening our bones and joints.

It helps us maintain a healthy body composition, decreases risk of arthritis, osteoporosis and injury. As well as all this, strength training improves insulin sensitivity, enhances lipid profiles, and reduces blood pressure and the risk of major diseases.

In short, exercise increases longevity. But not only does it extend our lives, most of all it gives us the quality of life to enjoy those extra years. Just think how much you will enjoy meeting those extra great-grandchildren! You are never too old to begin harnessing the power of this incredible fountain of youth.

Quality vs Quantity

For your body to get stronger it simply needs to be challenged at an adequate level for it to respond, and then be allowed sufficient time to recover before repeating the process.

To see the best strength results, it is important to add enough load or intensity to fire up both your fast and slow twitch muscle fibres, rather than doing lots of easy repetitions at a low load which have very little effect.

Adequate recovery is also vital between training sessions, as overtraining is a common problem which leads to plateaus in results and niggling injuries. For best results, let go of time wasting exercises and stick to compound movements that move several joints and work multiple muscles at the same time. This also gives you great functional strength for everyday life.

Stand Strong

Our posture both reflects and affects how we feel every day. Consider your posture as you read these words. How do you naturally hold your shoulders, your neck, how do you sit, stand and walk? Our bodies are made up of complex interconnected systems of fascia, tendons, ligaments and muscles which attach onto bone and enable us to move.

Repetitive movement patterns and body positions such as hunching over a computer, slouching in a chair or extending our head forward, often lead to areas of tightness, imbalance and pain. Be aware of your posture and discover ways to free yourself up by moving fluidly in all planes of motion and especially in opposing directions to common postures you adopt.

Harness the power of your posture to transform how you feel. You can instantly boost your mood and confidence simply by extending both arms above your head in a V and lifting your gaze. Try it out with a smile and see!

Build Resilience

Our resilience determines our ability to cope with the things that life throws at us. Strengthening your resilience is like taking out a personal insurance policy which will help you weather the storms of life. When times get tough you will be able to draw from your reserves of resilience and keep going.

We all experience stress in a range of forms including physical, mental and emotional. A certain amount of stress is positive, and is called eustress. It excites and motivates us to perform at our peak.

Once our stress levels go past this point however, we experience distress which impairs our ability and leaves us feeling overwhelmed. This further reduces our cognitive function and creates a negative spiral. You can increase your resilience in advance by intentionally including resilience boosting practises into your daily routines and learning how to reframe thoughts in a positive manner.

Strong Mind

You are the leader of your own life. When you have your own strong moral compass you are much less likely to be dragged off course by others. Rather you will stand firm and positively influence and lead those around you. Having a set of values and beliefs that serve you helps you to positively frame the way you see yourself and the world.

Self-belief comes from a strong sense of identity that is grounded in truth and self-acceptance.

The more you understand yourself, the more you can capitalise on your traits, strengths and personality style. This allows you to shine your light in the world.

Social Connection

All humans crave social connection with others. It is an essential human need to give and receive love and affection. Quality friendships boost health, happiness and longevity. The number of friends that we have is not that important, rather it's the quality of connection that we maintain and the shared moments and memories that greatly enhances our wellbeing. Having close friends who you can rely on and relax and be vulnerable with is vital.

Surround yourself with positive people that energise, inspire and uplift you. Take time to cultivate and strengthen those relationships by identifying and speaking their love language. If you have a spouse or partner, treasure them, thank them daily for the things you love and appreciate about them and never stop dating.

Restore

Breathe

Deep diaphragmatic breathing is one of the most effective ways to combat stress. Our breath is so closely linked to our emotions that it changes in accordance with how we're feeling. The great thing is that we can consciously adapt our breathing and in turn improve how we feel.

Breathing is the only part of our autonomic nervous system that we can influence. We can switch our breathing off auto-pilot by consciously taking full, deep, slow breaths which signal to our body that we are feeling relaxed, confident and in control. This practice shifts your body away from "fight or flight" mode, restores good digestion, aids immunity and assists fat burning. It also increases the fresh oxygen supply to the brain making you more alert and energised and helping you stay present.

Stay in Rhythm

Our bodies have natural ultradian rhythms throughout the day each with a 90-120 minute upswing when we can perform at our peak, interspersed with 10-15 minute downswings when the body and brain need to recharge and reset. Work in sync with these rhythms so you can feel and perform at your best.

Rather than pushing through the tired signals that indicate a downswing, take a few minutes to recharge. Having a short power nap or being still and calm allows the brain to file away information and prepare for the next peak.

At the very least create a change of state, for example from sitting to active or from writing to stretching.

The short break saves you time, making you more efficient overall as you will work with more creativity, accuracy and speed than before the break. Structure your day in sync with your body's rhythm. Complete high level tasks when you have the best energy and you will feel *in flow* throughout the day.

Sleep Well

Humans cannot live without sleep. Quality sleep is fundamental to our energy levels, mood and a wide range of internal body functions such as cell repair and rebuilding. Most adults need seven to nine hours of quality sleep to perform optimally. It is important to have a restful sleep environment that is dark, cool and free of clutter and technology.

Having a bedtime routine allows the body to wind down and the brain to let go of mental clutter, setting you up for quality deep sleep. Exercise during the day improves sleep, but it is best to avoid vigorous exercise or stimulants such as caffeine or alcohol in the evening. Dim the lights and avoid all screens within two hours of bedtime.

Stay in sync with your natural body clock and circadian rhythm by getting sunlight into your retina when you wake and also near midday. Go to bed and rise at similar times each day for optimal sleep.

Restorative Movement

An exercise routine that includes higher intensity fitness and strength training is great, but restorative movement is equally important for optimal health. People today find that they are increasingly stressed, so it is more important than ever to balance fast movement with slow, gentle movements which restore the body and mind and re-balance stress hormones.

Stretching and mobilising your muscles and connective tissue is essential to allow natural movement and body posture, which affects how you feel and function every day. Practise a regular restorative movement routine either on your own or in a class setting. It can be a fantastic way to start the day on the right foot. The time taken to slow your breathing and focus on connecting with how your body feels is hugely beneficial.

Trust

We all live with uncertainty. How we view it and deal with it depends on our outlook on life. Often we try to control things in our lives and feel overwhelmed when they don't go as we planned or expected them to. Because there is so much that we can't control, it is incredibly freeing to choose to trust that everything will work out for good and simply let go. In reality all we let go of is the illusion of control.

Worry and anxiety can create an incredible amount of angst for people yet neither helps improve the situation. Do what you can to change the things you can and let go of the rest. Consider what is really important and how you will reflect on today ten years from now. Sometimes we just need to "let go and let God".

We often worry so much about what others think of us or try to act in a certain way that we lose sight of who we truly are. Trust yourself to be yourself in the moment and accept that you are perfectly ok in your imperfection. You are enough.

Be Present

Living in the present moment allows us to experience life to the full. Often we spend so much time in our own heads stewing over the past or worrying about the future that we are distracted from enjoying the present moment with the people we love. Give yourself permission to be spontaneous, playful and to have fun. When your body walks into a room, make sure that your mind is there too rather than being focused on other things.

One of the quickest ways to become present is check in with how your body is feeling physically. Take a deep breath and be aware of your surroundings and the distant sounds. Reflect on how you feel.

Even when you experience strong emotions it is beneficial to acknowledge and sit with them. Participating and being fully present in life is like living life in full colour rather than just observing it in black and white.

Appendices

1. Freezer Storage Guide

Item	Time	Notes
Butter	6-9 months	As a block or cubed, tightly wrapped.
Cheese	6 months	As a block, cubed or grated, tightly wrapped.
Milk	3-6 months	Pour into portion size containers and allow room for expansion.
Yoghurt	1-2 months	Pour into portion size containers and allow room for expansion. Best used in sauces/soups.
Deli meats	2-3 months	Store sliced or diced in an airtight bag or container.
Bacon, ham and sausages	6 months	Store whole or diced in an airtight bag or container.
Beef, lamb and pork	Cooked 2-3 months Raw 6-8 months	Store whole, sliced, diced or minced in an airtight bag or container.
Fish	Cooked 6 months Raw 6-9 months	Store filleted in an airtight bag or container.
Chicken and poultry	Cooked 4 months Raw 9-12 months	Store whole, pieces or fillets in an airtight bag or container.
Prawns, scallops, squid rings	6-8 months	Store in an airtight bag or container.
Tofu	3-5 months	Drain off fluid, wrap tightly and place inside a container.
Nuts	1-2 years	Store in an airtight bag.
Bread	3-6 months	Slice, then store in an airtight bag. Use one slice at a time, or defrost an entire loaf at room temperature inside the bag to retain its moisture.
Wraps	6-8 months	Separate each wrap between baking paper and store in an airtight bag.
Rice, grains, pasta and noodles	4-6 months	Cook, cool down and portion out into airtight bags or containers.
Beans and pulses	9-12 months	Soak overnight, cook, cool down and portion out into airtight bags or containers.
Tomato paste or canned tomatoes	3 months	Spoon out into ice cube or muffin trays and freeze, then pop out to store in a bag/container
Casseroles	3-4 months	Cook until slightly under-done. Cool down then cover the top and store in its dish or transfer to a freezer container, allowing room for expansion.

Item	Time	Notes
Soups	6 months	Cool and pour out into portion sized containers, allowing room for expansion.
Stock	6 months	Cool and pour into meal size (1-2 cup) bags or containers. Or to use for deglazing pour into ice cube trays freeze then pop out to store in a bag/container.
Bananas	6 months	Remove skins and chop into quarters. Store in airtight bags or a container.
Avocados	4 months	De-stone and cut into halves or quarters and store in an airtight bag. Or mash or blend into a smooth paste and spoon into ice cube trays freeze then pop out to store in a bag/container.
Tomatoes	4 months	Remove the hollow where the stem attached and freeze them whole in airtight bags. The skins will easily peel of when defrosted. Good for use in casseroles and soups.
Onions	3-6 months	Chop and store in an airtight bag within another bag to prevent odours escaping.
Root vegetables	3 months	Boil or roast then either leave whole or mash/puree and scoop into portion sized containers.
Most other vegetables such as broccoli, cauliflower, carrots, green beans, peas, corn, asparagus and leafy greens	6-8 months	Wash then chop and blanch for 2-3 minutes under boiling water, chill under cold water. Allow to dry then portion into airtight bags.
Berries	6-8 months	Clean and allow to dry. Spread on trays to freeze then pour into airtight bags to store.
Stewed fruit	12 months	Cool stewed fruit. Spoon into ice cube or muffin trays and freeze, then pop out to store in a bag/container.
Garlic	10-12 months	Store whole cloves with skin on or off, or diced, in an airtight bag within another bag to prevent odours escaping.
Ginger root	10-12 months	Remove skin with a teaspoon, finely dice and place into ice cube trays. Top with water and freeze, then pop out to store in a bag/container.
Herbs	12 months	Chop and spoon into ice cube trays. Cover with water or stock and freeze, then pop out to store in a bag/container.
Lemon and Lime	12 months	Zest the rind and place into ice cube trays. Cover with the juice and freeze, then pop out to store in a bag/container. Or dry freeze zest on its own in an airtight bag.

2. Cooking Guide for Grains, Starches and Lentils

The below ingredients can be cooked by the absorption method. Cook them in a pot on the stove top with the recommended amounts of water from the table below. Salt the water to bring out the flavour. Bring the pot to the boil and allow it to simmer with the lid on for the times recommended.

The exceptions are: couscous which is almost instantly cooked, pasta which cooks in a larger amount of water with the excess being drained off at the end, and lentils which can be cooked with the lid off and which are best salted towards the end of the cooking process.

You may notice holes appear, avoid stirring as these act as steam vents which assist with even cooking. To check that your ingredient is cooked though, taste towards the end of the cook time as the final result will come down to your personal preference.

To one cup of:	Add this amount of water:	Bring to a boil, then simmer for:	Amount after cooking:
Couscous	1 cup	No need to cook, simply stir and leave covered for 2 minutes, then fluff with a fork and cover for another 2 minutes before serving.	2 cups
Wholemeal pasta	6 cups or more	8-12 minutes	Varies
Quinoa	2 cups	12-15 minutes Then remove from heat, let it sit for 5 minutes then fluff it up with a fork.	3 ½ cups
Bulgur wheat	2 cups	15-20 minutes	3 cups
Buck wheat	1 cup	20-25 minutes	2 cups
Brown rice, long grain	2 ½ cups	30-45 minutes	3 cups
Brown rice, short grain	2 ½ cups	40-50 minutes	3 cups
Black rice	3 cups	45-55 minutes	3 ½ cups
Red lentils	3 cups	10-12 minutes	3 cups
Yellow lentils	3 cups	12-15 minutes	3 cups
Brown lentils	3 cups	30-35 minutes	3 cups
Puy lentils	4 cups	35-40 minutes	4 cups

Tips

- Save time by starting with boiling water from the jug (kettle).
- If you want to speed the cooking process you can soak grains in advance.
- You can also cook up big batches and store them in the fridge to use over the next 2-3 days either cold in salads or reheated as part of a meal.

3. Your Guide to Soaking and Sprouting at Home

As mentioned in part II soaking nuts and seeds can make them more easily digested and improve their nutritional value by reducing phytic acid and releasing helpful enzymes. Soak raw nuts or seeds by rinsing in a sieve, then covering them with warm salted water and leaving them on the bench. After soaking, drain and rinse them and they are ready to use. If you prefer to store them, you can dry them out in a dehydrator or by spreading them on an oven tray and warming them at 50°C (120°F) for 2-3 hours. You can even make tasty activated nut mixtures by adding salt and spices such as turmeric, curry or paprika while drying.

This is a guide to the recommended soaking times:

Nut/Seed	Soak Time
Almonds	8-12 hours
Walnuts, Hazelnuts, Pecans	6-8 hours
Macadamias, Pinenuts Pumpkin Seeds (pepitas)	4-5 hours
Sunflower Seeds, Linseeds	3-4 hours
Cashews, Brazil Nuts	2-3 hours

Making your own sprouts at home is a simple process that takes little time and gives you delicious enzyme and nutrient rich sprouts to add to your salads, wraps, sandwiches, soups and curries. Good options for starting out are mung beans and whole lentils. You can also try adzuki beans, blue peas, chick peas or alfalfa, or any mixture that appeals.

Here is the process:

1. Rinse your dry beans or seeds thoroughly in a sieve or colander until clean.
2. Put them in a large jar no more than ¼ the way up and fill the jar with water. Leave it to soak overnight at room temperature.
3. Drain the water off. Rinse and drain again, then cover with a mesh lid or a piece of muslin cloth and store the jar at room temperature, upside down on a slight angle on top of a plate.
4. Rinse with water once or twice a day.
5. After 2-3 days your sprouts should be a good length. Put the jar upright in the fridge and use within a few days. Wash your sprouts as you would with other vegetables. Smell them before use to check they still smell fresh, if not discard them and start a new batch.
6. Note that for alfalfa seeds only use 2-3 tablespoons in a jar as they grow to take a lot of space. Also put them in a sunny spot for a couple of hours once sprouted so the leaflets can develop some chlorophyll and turn green. When you rinse them, the hulls will float to the top and can be removed.

Thanks

This book could not have happened without the help and support of many wonderful people. I now understand what a huge task it is to write and publish a book, and I am incredibly grateful to everyone who has believed in me and encouraged me every step of the way.

I thank God for His unending perfect love. Thanks to my mum and dad for everything. Thanks to Jean-Michel and Béatrice Cadoret for teaching me an appreciation of food like never before. Thanks to all of my family and friends for your love and support.

Huge thanks to my amazing hubby Morrie for all the sacrifices, for being an incredible home hero and allowing me time to write, for his flair with flavour and spices and critical review of the recipes, but most of all for believing in me and this project (I owe you many cups of tea). Thanks to my girls for getting excited about mummy's book and for being excellent tasters.

Thanks to Phil and Terri Thompson for editing the manuscript and knocking it into shape so beautifully. Thanks to Jessica Ferriter for editing it for an international audience. Thanks to Pene Ashby, Patrick Dye and Karyn Thompson for the detailed proofreading.

Thanks to the team of reviewers Dr Bill Sukala, John Polley, Candy Wegener, Richard Beddie, Leanne Mulcahy, Lynn Kirkland, Broni McSweeney, Wendy Sweet and Robyn Pearce for reading an advance copy and providing fantastic feedback. Special thanks to Wendy and Robyn for the extra proofreading and for all your support.

Thanks to Jacquie Ritchie for founding Bellyful NZ, a much needed charity which I am proud to support. Thanks Steph Fink for agreeing for me to partner with you to raise awareness for Bellyful NZ. (www.bellyful.org.nz)

Thanks to Natalie Sisson, Karen Tui Boyes, Natalie Cutler-Welsh, Francesca Storey, Debra Rock-Evans and Lise Layton for your wisdom and guidance behind the scenes. Thanks to John Durney for being incredibly accommodating with all of the printing requirements. Thanks to Philip Bruinette for the superb videography.

Huge thanks to my wonderful creative team. To Beth van Hulst for your incredible photographic skill, food styling prowess and for making every shoot fun to be a part of. To Alex McCarthy for the stunning cover design, for travelling to be there for the shoot and for such diligence throughout the creative process refining it multiple times to make it perfect. To Charlene Lucas for the amazing interior design, for taking my words and ideas and making them flow beautifully on paper, for your creative flair and never compromising on excellence at any stage. You have each gone above and beyond and I have loved working with you all.

Thanks to everyone that supported the kickstarter, I love your faith in the unseen! Thanks to all of my clients and my online community for being a part of the journey and for providing invaluable feedback at various stages.

Lastly, *thank you* to *YOU* for purchasing this copy and joining me to create a positive ripple in your world.

Final Words

So there you have it!

You now have your complete guide on how to eat mindfully and have a relaxed attitude to food, plus all the tips and tricks you need to make cooking at home simple and fuss-free. I hope that you feel inspired to discover the potential of your new, healthier life as you use the salad blueprints, set up your "freezer-library" and boost your real food in a positive way.

As you put these practical steps in to place, you truly will see a transformation in the way that you look and feel. Time and money invested in improving your health are always well spent, because great health underpins everything you do and allows you to enjoy life to the full.

The first step is to try it all out. Clear some space, plan your menu for the week (or use my ideal plan to start with), get your groceries, open up the recipes and enjoy the delicious journey! Make sure you download your free printable meal planning resources at www.realfoodlessfuss.com/resources

As with most things in life, it will get easier and easier with practice and before you know it prioritising real food in your life will be second nature for you.

Remember that this is about much more than just transforming your own health. Thank you for being part of this real food less fuss revolution and creating a positive ripple in your family, your community and your world.

I always love hearing people's feedback and success stories so feel free to drop me a line at www.LaurenParsons.co.nz/contact

Wishing you an abundance of health and happiness now and always.